Wilhelm Hauff

The Little Glass Man

And Other Stories

Wilhelm Hauff

The Little Glass Man
And Other Stories

ISBN/EAN: 9783337004811

Printed in Europe, USA, Canada, Australia, Japan

Cover: Foto ©Thomas Meinert / pixelio.de

More available books at **www.hansebooks.com**

THE

LITTLE GLASS MAN

THE
LITTLE GLASS MAN

AND OTHER STORIES

FROM THE GERMAN

OF

WILHELM HAUFF

ILLUSTRATED

NEW YORK: MACMILLAN & CO.

LONDON: T. FISHER UNWIN

1894

CONTENTS

HOW THE STORIES WERE FOUND

BY L. ECKENSTEIN

FAIRY QUEEN sat in her office drinking afternoon tea. Fairy Queen, thinking how she could please children best, had turned publisher. She had come to London, she had taken an office up a steep flight of stairs, and had sent out her fairies all over Europe in search of children's books. Off they had gone in all directions, and so many manuscripts and books had been sent in or brought back by them, that Fairy Queen published volume after volume of the Children's Library, and still there remained a lot of work to be done.

There she sat now thinking over the tales she had published and over those she was planning to publish, as the clock of St. Paul's slowly struck five. Fairy Queen poured out a last cup of tea ; she finished sorting a heap

of letters which she packed away in the
drawers of her writing-table, and listened
in the direction of the room next to hers.
There were steps on the stairs coming and
going.   Then there was a good deal of
banging about the room, and Fairy Queen's
ear caught snatches of a song.

In that room were stored books, and
manuscripts, and letters and brown paper
parcels, and there by the side of the big, big
waste-paper basket of Fairy Queen's publish-
ing firm, sat Gogul Mogul reading manuscripts.   Gogul Mogul was a long-legged
creature, with a tiny head, who had come
out of Fairyland to help publish tales suitable for child readers.   He was devoted to
Fairy Queen, and read through piles and
piles of manuscript with great perseverance,
though he frequently groaned, longing to be
back in Fairyland.

But he was not groaning now.   As Fairy
Queen opened the door calling to him, he
was lightly dancing a double shuffle and
waving a telegram to the tune.   At sight of
her he burst into a joyous laugh.

'Her absence need not cast a shadow on
us all,' he cried ; 'the fairy from Germany
is on her way home.   She telegraphs to me
from Dover ; she will be here in time for the
fairies' meeting.   And having passed the
seas and crossed the sands, she found the
story of the Little Glass Man at last.'

'A good thing, a good thing,' said Fairy Queen, taking the telegram; 'as it is, I have lost all patience with her. From France, from Ireland, from Greece, even from Russia, numbers of tales have arrived. And from Germany, so much nearer to us, so much more literary, nothing comes. Just as though there were not plenty of fairy tales to be found there! But I have no doubt she has wasted so much time looking for these special stories, just because you had set your heart on having them.'

'Upon my word,' Gogul Mogul said. And he jumped over his toes, a feat he was fond of performing, serenely smiling at the large blot of ink which ornamented his forefinger.

'Of course you will meet her at the station,' said Fairy Queen; 'see her home, and call for her again in a cab. The meeting begins at nine; all the fairies who are in town will be there. And mind you do not keep us waiting as you did last month!'

Her tone was severe; but Gogul Mogul went on smiling his sweetest smile, while he muttered to himself—

'Then skilful most, when most severely judged,
But chance it not.'

A few hours later daylight had passed away and a bright moon looked down into the thronged thoroughfare of Holborn, putting to shame the yellow lights of the gas lamps and the glare of the few shop windows that were lit up by electric light.   Into side courts and up winding alleys the moon made her way, and poured down full into a narrow passage up which ladies' figures, bundled in ulsters and shawls, were hurrying in twos and threes.

Under an arched doorway they disappeared.   The moon could not look round the corner, but above there was a row of arched stone windows.   She looked in at these into a long large wainscotted old hall, and there she found those figures and knew them again.

I doubt if you would have known them. I should not myself but that I had been helping downstairs in the cloak-room, taking hats and wraps and ulsters, even one pair of goloshes, and mixing them up for the surprise of seeing what lovely creatures came out from those dark clothes.   Have you ever seen a butterfly squeeze out of a chrysalis, I wonder?   Have you seen those shining creatures shake themselves free from their dark covering, take flight, and vanish away?   But those lovely creatures whose cloaks I helped to ticket could not vanish away from me altogether.   Like the moon, I managed to find them again.

For I knew of a small window upstairs from which one could overlook the old hall. When there were smoking concerts this window was open for ventilation to let out the smoke ; to-night it should be open for me to peep in. So when the old lady in the cloak-room said she required my help no longer, she thought it was time for me to go to bed ; I said 'Thank you,' and went upstairs and made my way along the passages to the small window, and sat close to it and looked down into the old hall.

Oh, the colour, the movement, the loveliness of it all ! I once went to a pantomime and saw the Transformation Scene with all the fairies. It was very beautiful and a little like what I saw now. Only there the fairies were all made up with painted faces, and curls which had not grown on their heads, while here you could see at a glance that everything was quite real. And they were so lovely, these fairies ! I made myself comfortable at the window, no one could see me from below. Only the moon from the big window opposite stared me full in the face. 'No matter what *you* think,' I said, nodding at her ; 'don't *you* talk about inquisitiveness. Why there isn't a window or a cranny but you take a peep in if you get the chance !'

Down below, at one end of the hall, there was a raised platform ; on this, in the largest of the chairs, sat Fairy Queen with a crown on her head and a long silver train. A few other fairies, all with long trains, sat by her,

and the rest moved about in the hall.   In
one corner, just below where I sat, there was
a long table, on which were set out plates with
pasties and sweets and sandwiches ; there
were coloured glasses also and flagons of wine.
Near the table stood Gogul Mogul greeting
the fairies as they arrived and handing them
refreshments.   He was dressed in green
tights, his hair stood up in a great mop.
Among all those ladies he was the only
gentleman ; but he knew his importance,
and he looked it.

'Oh yes, she has come,' I heard him say
in answer to inquiries ; 'what heart could
wish for more ! she is without, putting herself straight.   Did you say raspberry tart or
cherry tart ?' he asked, turning to a fairy.
And taking up a flagon, he quoted—

> ' Here plenty's liberal horn shall pour,
>   Of fruits for thee a copious shower.'

Suddenly there was a stir, the door had
opened and a fairy came in dressed in the
bluest of blues.   Gogul Mogul went up to
her ; she came to the table and ate a sandwich ; then he led her by the hand to the
upper end of the room, where Fairy Queen
and the other grand fairies rose to receive
her.   They talked of her long absence, then
of other things.   But I was not listening ;
I was watching Gogul Mogul, who had come
back to the refreshment table, where, all the

fairies having been helped, he proceeded to help himself. I have seen school-boys in bun shops, and school-girls settling down to a feast of chocolate creams ; in these I have sometimes joined myself. But never before, never since, did I see the like of Gogul Mogul. Sandwich after sandwich, tart after tart, he put into his mouth ; there was no choosing, no hesitation, no pause, till every bit of the food off the dishes had gone. And then—it sounds nonsense, and no one will believe it possible who has not seen it done—he turned up the cloth at one end of the table, then at the other, and went on rolling and rolling it up over plates and dishes and glasses and flagons, till there was nothing left but a small napkin, which he squeezed into the breast-pocket slit of his tight green clothes.

I looked up and straight at the moon, who seemed to be smiling. ' Is it a dream,' I thought, ' is it a practical joke, or is it really a meeting of the Women's Gossip Revival Society, as they said downstairs ?'

The Blue Fairy was now sitting on the platform, all the other fairies too had taken seats. Gogul Mogul, the wonderful Gogul Mogul, who well deserved the title of Food Destroyer to Her Majesty, sauntered up to the platform, where he sat down by the side of Fairy Queen.

Fairy Queen then rose and said : ' This

night being the Full Moon we have met as usual to hear what the fairies have to report about children's books and child-readers; how the children have liked the stories, and what they think of them.   But as the Blue Fairy has just arrived from Germany, where she has been so long, I propose to call on her to tell us some of her adventures.'

There was a great clapping of hands at this.   Gogul Mogul stood up, bowed to the Blue Fairy, and said: 'A feast of reason and a flow of soul!' at which there was renewed clapping of hands.

The Blue Fairy hesitated, she fingered the gold spangles of her dress, she shook back her curls.   Then she began:

'Germany is a wonderful country.   It is very big as you know, and very different in places; the parts I like best are the large forests which extend uphill and downhill for many many miles.   We all hope to go back to Fairyland some day, but next to going there we could not do better than settle in one of these German forests; with the squirrels playing about, and the birds singing, and the little streams bubbling between the moss-grown rocks, I really felt quite at home there.   The folk live in the queerest of houses, and are dressed in the queerest of clothes; and there can be nothing funnier than the dear little children, who come a long distance over the hills to school, walking

barefoot, and who sit down outside the
schoolhouse and put on their stockings and
shoes before they go in, as if wearing shoes
and stockings were part of doing lessons.
Well, I went to stay in the Black Forest
first ; Gogul Mogul told me it was there I
must go to hear about the Little Glass Man.
I believe he knew him as a boy when the
Little Glass Man used to visit in Fairyland.
But I travelled about on coaches painted a
bright yellow, I stayed about in old-fashioned
sunny village inns, I heard about many
wonderful things, but I could not find out
anything about the Little Glass Man. Had
he left those parts, had people forgotten
about him ?

‘One afternoon I had been in a saw-mill
watching the saw go up and down through
the long pine-wood trunk which slowly
moved along to meet it, to the sound of the
splashing wheel outside going round and
round. Every time the saw had cut through
the length of the trunk it stopped, there was
a great rush of water outside, a little bell
was set tinkling, and then the sawyer, or the
saw-miller, as they call him over there, wound
the trunk back and set the saw so as to cut
the next plank, and then the whole thing
was again set going. It was curious watching the sawdust jerked up, and the huge
block of timber cut lengthwise into so many
planks, and the miller going in and out over

the sawdust.   I felt quite sorry when at last
he stopped the little bell without setting
the saw going again, and came and stood
by me.

'Then we talked about this and that, and
I asked him about the Little Glass Man; he
must know so many woodmen who felled the
trees and brought the timber to the mill;
had they ever met him?

'The miller was a big rough man with a
stubbly beard; I don't know if he was at all
deaf, but when he spoke it was so loud that
he must have thought me dull of hearing.

'"Take my advice," he said, "if you
want to know about the country go into the
town.   Don't expect us to know about Little
Glass Men, or other little men; we don't care
for such things.   But in the town you are
sure to find all about it stored away in some
book.   Take my advice, go into a town; it
is there that you find out about things in the
country."

'Was he right? I wondered as I walked
home that night.   I could not believe it, so
I stayed on in the Black Forest till it was
time to come home, but without ever hearing
of the Little Glass Man.   I was on the rail-
road again.   It was early one morning
when we stopped at a station; there was no
train for two hours, so I took a walk into
the town.   There was a clear, fast-flowing
river below, and in the distance again such

wonderful wooded hills. I went into a shop
and asked for some writing-paper.

'The gentleman who brought it out had
on the shabbiest of coats, but on his head
there was an embroidered velvet cap, and
his slippers too were embroidered. Only
his toes were stuck inside these, and he
moved about the shop slowly so as not to
leave them behind.

' "And what is the name of that wood
yonder?—those hills, I mean?—those wooded
heights?—that mountain range?" I asked,
trying word after word, and at last standing
in the doorway and pointing at the hills
opposite, while he blankly stared at me.

' "Where can you be from that you should
not know?" he said at last.

' "I am from England," I said rather hotly,
"from London, a small place you may have
heard of."

'He nodded, "Oh yes, I know. You
have not come all that way alone; surely a
lady by herself . . ."

' "Oh yes I have," I said, "and I have a
good mind to go up among those hills by
myself too; perhaps some one up there
might tell me what they are called."

' "Look here," he said, "if you really
mean to go, let me lend you my map. I
have got such a splendid one. And I shan't
be using it for months, as there is no one to
mind the shop for me."

'He brought it out of a drawer and un-folded it, while I stared in my turn.

'"You see," he said, "that is the highest point; now be sure you don't miss seeing that. You see Forsthaus Diana marked; well there is the inn, that spot close to it. That is where all those wonderful stories were told."

'"What stories?" I said; "nothing about the Little Glass Man, I suppose?"

'He went to the back of the shop and fumbled about.

'"Yes, of course, about the Little Glass Man, and about the Golden Florin," he said; "even if you live in an out-of-the-way place like London, you must have heard of them. Here is the book; stories by Hauff. Dear me, to think that my father met the man more than once who stored up all these treasures! You can take the book as well as the map, if you like; if you are not coming back this way you can send them by any one who is."

'There was no chair in the shop, I had to support myself against the counter, I felt so overcome with having found the story at last. The gentleman went on pointing out the best way to go, and what I must see, and after half an hour it was all settled, my luggage was to be sent up one way and I was to go another.

'"I am glad you will see the old inn

standing where the stories were told," he said, "and you will be quite comfortable at the forest-house Diana. If I were you I should tell the lady-forester at once that you are an English girl, and no Nihilist; that is what she is sure to think if she sees a girl travelling about by herself. Tell her I sent you there, and give my love to her niece Malchen, a wild little girl but a good one, I feel sure, whatever they say to the contrary."'

At this point of her narrative the Blue Fairy stopped. There was a pause.

'Well?' said Gogul Mogul. 'Go on, please go on,' the fairies called in the audience.

'There is nothing more to tell,' said the Blue Fairy; 'the story of the Little Glass Man was found. I read it through the next afternoon, sitting in the garden of the inn where the student had originally told it. Then I went back into the forest-house Diana, and sat chatting in the kitchen with the lady-forester while the apples and potatoes for the pigs were stewing, and Malchen sat by eating sour milk from a great earthenware bowl. But of course that has nothing to do with the finding of the stories. Only it was so enjoyable up there, it was so delightful walking with that splendid map, and reading those stories, and making friends with a charcoal-burner who was quite like Peter Munk, and looking on while huge bits of timber were felled, that I stayed on and on.   Only of course there was the work of translating the stories into English.'

Again the Blue Fairy stopped ; there was prolonged cheering and clapping of hands. It was Fairy Queen who spoke next :

'All this is very interesting,' she said, 'and so, I feel sure, is a great deal more which the Blue Fairy could tell us about Germany.   But she has been travelling all day, she must be tired, we must not ask for more to-night ; only I am sure you must all be wanting to hear the story about this Little Glass Man.   As for myself, I am most anxious to hear what he was like and what he did.   As the fairy has translated the story into English, and Gogul Mogul is sure to have the manuscript about him, I propose calling on him to read it to us.'

There was long and loud cheering at this among the fairies.   Gogul Mogul fumbled first in one pocket, then in another ; at last he brought out a roll of manuscript and began as follows :

THE LITTLE GLASS MAN

THOSE who travel through Swabia should always remember to cast a passing glance into the Schwarzwald,[1] not so much for the sake of the trees (though pines are not found everywhere in such prodigious numbers, nor of such a surpassing height), as for the sake of the people, who show a marked difference from all others in the neighbourhood. They are taller than ordinary men, broad-shouldered, strong-limbed, and it seems as if the bracing air which blows through the pines in the morning, had allowed them, from their youth upwards, to breathe more freely, and had given them a clearer eye and a firmer, though ruder, mind than the inhabitants of the valleys and plains. The strong contrast they form to the people living without the limits of the

[1] The Black Forest.

"Wald," consists, not merely in their bearing and stature, but also in their manners and costume. Those of the Schwarzwald of the Baden territory dress most handsomely; the men allow their beards to grow about the chin just as nature gives it; and their black jackets, wide trousers, which are plaited in small folds, red stockings, and painted hats surrounded by a broad brim, give them a strange, but somewhat grave and noble appearance. Their usual occupations are the manufacturing of glass, and the so-called Dutch clocks, which they carry about for sale over half the globe.

Another part of the same race lives on the other side of the Schwarzwald; but their occupations have made them contract manners and customs quite different from those of the glass manufacturers. Their *Wald* supplies their trade; felling and fashioning their pines, they float them through the *Nagold* into the *Neckar*, from thence down the Rhine as far as Holland; and near the sea the *Schwarzwälder* and their long rafts are well known. Stopping at every town which is situated along the river, they wait proudly for purchasers of their beams and planks; but the strongest and longest beams they sell at a high price to Mynheers, who build ships of them. Their trade has accustomed them to a rude and roving life, their pleasure consisting in drifting down the stream on their timber, their sorrow in wandering back again along the shore. Hence the difference in their costume from that of the glass manufacturers. They wear jackets of a dark linen cloth, braces a hand-breadth wide, displayed over the chest, and trousers of black leather, from the pocket of which a brass rule sticks out as a badge of honour; but their pride and joy are their boots, which are probably the largest that are worn in any part of the world, for they may be drawn two spans above the knee, and the raftsmen may walk about in water at three feet depth without getting their feet wet.

It is but a short time ago that the belief in hobgoblins of the wood prevailed among the inhabitants, this foolish superstition having been eradicated only in modern times. But the singularity about these hobgoblins who are said to haunt the Schwarzwald, is, that they also wear the different costumes of the people. Thus it is affirmed of the Little Glass Man, a kind little sprite three feet and a half high, that he never shows himself except in a painted little hat with a broad brim, a doublet, white trousers, and red stockings; while Dutch Michel, who haunts the other side of the forest, is said to be a gigantic, broad-shouldered fellow wearing the dress of a raftsman; and many who have seen him

C

say they would not like to pay for the
calves whose hides it would require to make
one pair of his boots, affirming that, without
exaggeration, a man of the middle height
may stand in one of them with his head
only just peeping out.

The following strange adventure with
these spirits is said to have once befallen a
young Schwarzwälder:—There lived a widow
in the Schwarzwald whose name was Frau
Barbara Munk; her husband had been a
charcoal-burner, and after his death she had
by degrees prevailed upon her boy, who was
now sixteen years old, to follow his father's
trade. Young Peter Munk, a sly fellow,
submitted to sit the whole week near the
smoking stack of wood, because he had seen
his father do the same; or, black and sooty
and an abomination to the people as he was,
to drive to the nearest town and sell his
charcoal. Now a charcoal-burner has
much leisure for reflection, about himself
and others; and when Peter Munk was
sitting by his stack, the dark trees around
him, as well as the deep stillness of the
forest, disposed his heart to tears, and to
an unknown secret longing. Something
made him sad, and vexed him, without his
knowing exactly what it was. At length,
however, he found out the cause of his vexa-
tion,—it was his condition. 'A black,
solitary charcoal-burner,' he said to himself;

'it is a wretched life. How much more are the glass manufacturers, and the clock-makers regarded ; and even the musicians, on a Sunday evening ! And when Peter Munk appears washed, clean, and dressed out in his father's best jacket with the silver buttons and bran - new red stockings — if then, any one walking behind him, thinks to himself, " I wonder who that smart fellow is ? " admiring, all the time, my stockings and stately gait ;—if then, I say, he passes me and looks round, will he not say, " Why, it is only Peter Munk, the charcoal-burner" ?'

The raftsmen also on the other side of the wood were an object of envy to him. When these giants of the forest came over in their splendid clothes, wearing about their bodies half a hundredweight of silver, either in buckles, buttons, or chains, stand-ing with sprawling legs and consequential look to see the dancing, swearing in Dutch, and smoking Cologne clay pipes a yard long, like the most noble Mynheers, then he pictured to himself such a raftsman as the most perfect model of human happiness. But when these fortunate men put their hands into their pocket, pulled out hand-fuls of thalers and staked a Sechsbätzner piece upon the cast of a die, throwing their five or ten florins to and fro, he was almost mad and sneaked sorrowfully home to his hut. Indeed he had seen some of these

gentlemen of the timber trade, on many a
holy-day evening, lose more than his poor
old father had gained in the whole year.
There were three of these men in particular
of whom he knew not which to admire
most. The one was a tall stout man with
ruddy face, who passed for the richest man
in the neighbourhood; he was usually
called 'fat Hezekiel.' Twice every year he
went with timber to Amsterdam, and had
the good luck to sell it so much dearer than
the others that he could return home in a
splendid carriage, while they had to walk.
The second was the tallest and leanest man
in the whole *Wald*, and was usually called
'the tall Schlurker'; it was his extraordinary
boldness that excited Munk's envy, for he
contradicted people of the first importance,
took up more room than four stout men, no
matter how crowded the inn might be,
setting either both his elbows upon the
table, or drawing one of his long legs on
the bench; yet, notwithstanding all this,
none dared to oppose him, since he had a
prodigious quantity of money. The third
was a handsome young fellow, who being
the best dancer far around, was called 'the
king of the dancing-room.' Originally poor,
he had been servant to one of the timber
merchants, when all at once he became
immensely rich; for which some accounted
by saying he had found a potful of money

under an old pine tree, while others asserted that he had fished up in the Rhine, near Bingen, a packet of gold coins with the spear which these raftsmen sometimes throw at the fish as they go along in the river, that packet being part of the great 'Niebe-lungenhort,' which is sunk there. However this might be, the fact of his suddenly becoming rich caused him to be looked upon as a prince by young and old.

Often did poor Peter Munk the coal-burner think of these three men when sitting alone in the pine forest. All three indeed had one great fault, which made them hated by everybody; this was their insatiable avarice, their heartlessness towards their debtors and towards the poor, for the Schwarzwälder are naturally a kind-hearted people. However, we all know how it is in these matters; though they were hated for their avarice, yet they commanded respect on account of their money, for who but they could throw away thalers, as if they could shake them from the pines?

'This will do no longer,' said Peter one day to himself, when he felt very melancholy, it being the morrow after a holiday, when everybody had been at the inn; 'if I don't soon thrive I shall make away with myself; oh that I were as much looked up to and as rich as the stout Hezekiel, or as bold and powerful as the tall Schlurker, or as renowned as the king of the dancing-room, and could, like him, throw thalers instead of kreutzers to the musicians! I wonder where the fellow gets his money!' Reflecting upon all the different means by which money may be got, he could please himself with none, till at length he thought of the tales of those people who, in times of old, had become rich through the Dutchman Michel, or the Little Glass Man. During his father's lifetime other poor people often came to call, and then their conversation was generally about rich persons, and the means by which they had come by their riches; in these discourses the Little Glass Man frequently played a conspicuous part. Now, if Peter strained his memory a little, he could almost recall the short verse which one must repeat near the Tannenbühl in the heart of the forest, to make the sprite appear. It began as follows—

' Keeper of wealth in the forest of pine,
Hundreds of years are surely thine :
Thine is the tall pine's dwelling place—'

But he might tax his memory as much as he pleased, he could remember no more of it. He often thought of asking some aged person what the whole verse was. However, a certain fear of betraying his thoughts kept him back, and moreover he concluded that the legend of the Little Glass Man could not be very generally known, and that but few were acquainted with the incantation, since there were not many rich persons in the Wald ;—if it were generally known, why had not his father, and other poor people, tried their luck ? At length, however, he one day got his mother to talk about the little man, and she told him what he knew already, as she herself remembered only the first line of the verse ; but she added that the sprite would show himself only to those who had been born on a Sunday, between eleven and two o'clock. He was, she said, quite fit for evoking him, as he was born at twelve o'clock at noon ; if he but knew the verse.

When Peter Munk heard this he was almost beside himself with joy and desire to try the adventure. It appeared to him enough to know part of the verse, and to be born on a Sunday, for the Little Glass Man to show himself. Consequently when he one day had sold his charcoal, he did not light a new stack, but put on his father's holiday jacket, his new red stockings, and best hat, took his blackthorn stick, five feet long, into his hand, and bade farewell to his mother, saying, ' I must go to the magistrate in the town, for we shall soon have to draw lots who is to be soldier, and therefore I wish to impress once more upon him that you are a widow, and I am your only son.' His mother praised his resolution ; but he started

for the Tannenbühl. This lies on the highest
point of the Schwarzwald, and not a village
or even a hut was found, at that time, for two
leagues around, for the superstitious people
believed it was haunted ; they were even
very unwilling to fell timber in that part,
though the pines were tall and excellent, for
often the axes of the wood-cutters had flown
off the handle into their feet, or the trees
falling suddenly, had knocked the men
down, and either injured or even killed them ;
moreover, they could have used the finest
trees from there only for fuel, since the raftsmen never would take a trunk from the
Tannenbühl as part of a raft, there being a
tradition that both men and timber would
come to harm if they had a tree from that
spot on the water. Hence the trees there
grew so dense and high that it was almost
night at noon. When Peter Munk approached the place, he felt quite awe-
stricken, hearing neither voice nor footstep
except his own ; no axe resounded, and
even the birds seemed to shun the darkness
amidst the pines.

Peter Munk had now reached the highest
point of the Tannenbühl, and stood before a
pine of enormous girth, for which a Dutch
shipbuilder would have given many hundred
florins on the spot. 'Here,' said he, 'the
treasure - keeper (Schatzhauser) no doubt
lives ;' and pulling off his large hat, he

made a low bow before the tree, cleared his
throat, and said with a trembling voice, ' I
wish you a good evening, Mr. Glass Man.'
But receiving no answer, and all around
remaining silent as before, he thought it
would probably be better to say the verse,
and therefore murmured it forth. On repeating the words he saw, to his great
astonishment, a singular and very small
figure peep forth from behind the tree. It
seemed to him as if he had beheld the Little
Glass Man, just as he was described ; the
little black jacket, red stockings, hat, all
even to the pale, but fine shrewd countenance
of which the people talked so much, he
thought he had seen. But alas, as quickly
as it had peeped forth, as quickly it had
disappeared again. ' Mr. Glass Man,' cried
Peter Munk, after a short hesitation, ' pray
don't make a fool of me ; if you fancy that
I have not seen you, you are vastly mistaken ;
I saw you very well peeping forth from
behind the tree.' Still no answer ; only at
times he fancied he heard a low, hoarse
tittering behind the tree. At length his
impatience conquered this fear, which had
still restrained him, and he cried, ' Wait, you
little rascal, I will have you yet.' At the
same time he jumped behind the tree, but
there was no Schatzhauser, and only a pretty
little squirrel was running up the tree.

Peter Munk shook his head ; he saw he

had succeeded to a certain degree in the incantation, and that he perhaps only wanted one more rhyme to the verse to evoke the Little Glass Man ; he tried over and over again, but could not think of anything.   The squirrel showed itself on the lowest branches of the tree, and seemed to encourage or perhaps to mock him.   It trimmed itself, it rolled its pretty tail, and looked at him with its cunning eyes.   At length he was almost afraid of being alone with this animal ; for sometimes it seemed to have a man's head and to wear a three-cornered hat, sometimes to be quite like another squirrel, with the exception only of having red stockings and black shoes on its hind feet.   In short, it was a merry little creature, but still Peter felt an awe, fancying that all was not right.

Peter now went away with more rapid strides than he had come.   The darkness of the forest seemed to become blacker and blacker ; the trees stood closer to each other, and he began to be so terrified that he ran off in a trot, and only became more tranquil when he heard dogs bark at a distance, and soon after descried the smoke of a hut through the trees.   But on coming nearer and seeing the dress of the people, he found that having taken the contrary direction, he had got to the raftsmen instead of the glass-makers.   The people living in the hut were wood-cutters, consisting of an aged man with his son, who was the owner, and some grown-up grandchildren. They received Peter Munk, who begged a night's quarter, hospitably enough without asking his name or residence ; they gave him cider to drink, and in the evening a large black cock, the best meal in the Schwarzwald, was served up for supper.

After this meal the housewife and her daughters took their distaffs and sat round a large pine torch, which the boys fed with the finest rosin ; the host with his guest sat smoking and looking at the women ; while the boys were busy carving wooden spoons and forks. The storm was howling and raging through the pines in the forest without, and now and then very heavy blasts were heard, and it was as if whole trees were breaking off and crashing down. The fearless youths were about to run out to witness this terrific and beautiful spectacle, but their grandfather kept them back with a stern look and these words : 'I would not advise any of you,' cried he, 'to go now outside the door ; by heavens he never would return, for Michel the Dutchman is building this night a new raft in the forest.'

The younger of them looked at him with astonishment, having probably heard before of Michel, but they begged their grandpapa to tell them some interesting story of him. Peter Munk, who had heard but confused stories of Michel the Dutchman on the other side of the forest, joined in this request, asking the old man who and where' he was. 'He is the lord of the forest,' was the answer; 'and from your not having heard this at your age, it follows that you must be a native of those parts just beyond the Tannenbühl, or perhaps still more distant. But I will tell you all I know, and how the story goes about him. A hundred years ago or thereabouts, there were far and wide no people more upright in their dealings than the Schwarzwälder, at least so my grandfather used to tell me. Now, since there is so much money in the country, the people are dishonest and bad. The young fellows dance and riot on Sundays, and swear to such a degree that it is horrible to hear them; whereas formerly it was quite different, and I have often said and now say, though he should look in through the window, that the Dutchman Michel is the cause of all this depravity. A hundred years ago there lived a very rich timber merchant who had many servants; he carried his trade far down the Rhine and was very prosperous, being a pious man. One evening a person such as he had never seen came to his door; his dress was like that of the young fellows of the Schwarzwald, but he was full a head taller than any of them, and no one had ever thought there could be such a giant.

He asked for work, and the timber merchant, seeing he was strong, and able to carry great weights, agreed with him about the wages and took him into his service. He found Michel to be a labourer such as he had never yet had; for in felling trees he was equal to three ordinary men, and when six men were pulling at one end of a trunk he would carry the other end alone. After having been employed in felling timber for six months, he came one day before his master, saying, "I have now been cutting wood long enough here, and should like to see what becomes of my trunks; what say you to letting me go with the rafts for once?" To which his master replied, "I have no objection, Michel, to your seeing a little of the world; to be sure I want strong men like yourself to fell the timber, and on the river all depends upon skill; but, nevertheless, be it for this time as you wish."

'Now the float with which Michel was to go consisted of eight rafts, and in the last there were some of the largest beams. But what then? The evening before starting the tall Michel brought eight beams to the water, thicker and longer than had ever been seen, and he carried every one of them as easily upon his shoulder as if it had been a rowing-pole, so that all were amazed. Where he had felled them, no one knows to this day. The heart of the timber merchant was leaping with joy when he saw this, calculating what these beams would fetch; but Michel said, "Well, these are for me to travel on; with those chips I should not be able to get on at all." His master was going to make him a present of a pair of boots, but throwing them aside, Michel brought out a pair the largest that had ever been seen, and my grandfather assured me they weighed a hundred pounds and were five feet long.

'The float started; and if Michel had before astonished the wood-cutters, he perfectly astonished the raftsmen; for his raft, instead of drifting slowly down the river as they thought it would, by reason of the immense beams, darted on like an arrow, as soon as they came into the Neckar. If the river took a turn, or if they came to any part where they had a difficulty in keeping the middle stream, or were in danger of running aground, Michel always jumped into the water, pushing his float either to the right or to the left, so that he glided past without danger. If they came to a part where the river ran straight, Michel often sprang to the foremost raft, and making all put up their poles, fixed his own enormous pole in the sand, and by one push made the float dart along, so that it seemed as if the land, trees, and villages were flying by them. Thus they came in half the time they generally took to Cologne on the Rhine, where

they formerly used to sell their timber.
Here Michel said, "You are but sorry merchants and know nothing of your advantage.
Think you these Colognese want all the
timber from the Schwarzwald for themselves ?
I tell you no, they buy it of you for half its
value, and sell it dear to Holland. Let us
sell our small beams here, and go to Holland
with the large ones ; what we get above the
ordinary price is our own profit."

'Thus spoke the subtle Michel, and the
others consented ; some because they liked
to go and see Holland, some for the sake of
the money. Only one man was honest, and
endeavoured to dissuade them from putting
the property of their master in jeopardy or
cheating him out of the higher price. However, they did not listen to him and forgot
his words, while Michel forgot them not.
So they went down the Rhine with the
timber, and Michel, guiding the float, soon
brought them to Rotterdam. Here they
were offered four times as much as at
Cologne, and particularly the large beams
of Michel fetched a very high sum. When
the Schwarzwälders beheld the money, they
were almost beside themselves with joy.
Michel divided the money, putting aside
one-fourth for their master, and distributing
the other three among the men. And now
they went into the public-houses with sailors
and other rabble, squandering their money

in drinking and gambling ; while the honest
fellow who had dissuaded them was sold by
Michel to a slave-trader, and has never been
heard of since.   From that time forward
Holland was a paradise to the fellows from
the Schwarzwald, and the Dutchman Michel
their king.   For a long time the timber
merchants were ignorant of this proceeding,
and before people were aware, money, swearing, corrupt manners, drunkenness and
gambling were imported from Holland.

'When the thing became known, Michel
was nowhere to be found, but he was not
dead ; for a hundred years he has been
haunting the forest, and is said to have
helped many in becoming rich at the cost of
their souls of course : more I will not say.
This much, however, is certain, that to the
present day, in boisterous nights, he finds
out the finest pines in the Tannenbühl where
people are not to fell wood ; and my father
has seen him break off one of four feet
diameter, as he would break a reed.   Such
trees he gives to those who turn from the
right path and go to him ; at midnight they
bring their rafts to the water and he goes to
Holland with them.   If I were lord and king
in Holland, I would have him shot, for all the
ships that have but a single beam of Michel's,
must go to the bottom.   Hence it is that
we hear of so many shipwrecks ; if it were
not so, how could a beautiful, strong ship as

large as a church go down. But as often as Michel fells a pine in the forest during a boisterous night, one of his old ones starts from its joints, the water enters, and the ship is lost, men and all. So far goes the legend of the Dutchman Michel; and true it is that all the evil in the Schwarzwald dates from him. Oh! he can make one rich,' added the old man mysteriously; 'but I would have nothing from him; I would at no price be in the shoes of fat Hezekiel and the long Schlurker. The king of the dancing-room, too, is said to have made himself over to him.'

The storm had abated during the narrative of the old man; the girls timidly lighted their lamps and retired, while the men put a sackful of leaves upon the bench by the stove as a pillow for Peter Munk, and wished him good-night.

Never in his life had Peter such heavy dreams as during this night; sometimes he fancied the dark gigantic Michel was tearing the window open and reaching in with his monstrous long arm a purse full of gold pieces, which jingled clearly and loudly as he shook them; at another time he saw the little friendly Glass Man riding upon a huge green bottle about the room, and thought he heard again the same hoarse laughter as in the Tannenbühl; again something hummed into his left ear the following verse—

D

> ' In Holland I wot,
> There's gold to be got,
> Small price for a lot,
> Who would have it not ? '

Again he heard in his right ear the song of the Schatzhauser in the green forest, and a soft voice whispered to him, 'Stupid Coal-Peter, stupid Peter Munk, you cannot find a rhyme with "place," and yet are born on a Sunday at twelve o'clock precisely. Rhyme, dull Peter, rhyme !'

He groaned, he wearied himself to find a rhyme, but never having made one in his life, his trouble in his dream was fruitless. When he awoke the next morning with the first dawn, his dream seemed strange to him ; he sat down at the table with his arms crossed, and meditated upon the whisperings that were still ringing in his ears. He said to himself, ' Rhyme, stupid Peter, rhyme,' knocking his forehead with his finger, but no rhyme would come. While still sitting in this mood, looking gloomily down before him and thinking of a rhyme with 'place,' he heard three men passing outside and going into the forest, one of whom was singing—

> ' I stood upon the brightest place,
> I gazed upon the plain,
> And then—oh then—I saw that face,
> I never saw again.'

These words flashed like lightning through Peter's ear, and hastily starting up, he rushed out of the house, thinking he was mistaken in what he had heard, ran after the three fellows and seized, suddenly and rudely, the singer by the arm, crying at the same time, 'Stop, friend, what was it you rhymed with "place"? Do me the favour to tell me what you were singing.'

'What possesses you, fellow?' replied the Schwarzwälder. 'I may sing what I like; let go my arm, or——'

'No, you shall tell me what you were singing,' shouted Peter, almost beside himself, clutching him more tightly at the same time. When the other two saw this, they were not long in falling foul upon poor Peter with their large fists, and belabouring him till the pain made him release the third, and he sank exhausted upon his knees.

'Now you have your due,' said they, laughing; 'and mark you, madcap, never again stop people like us upon the highway.'

'Woe is me!' replied Peter with a sigh, 'I shall certainly recollect it. But now that I have had the blows, you will oblige me by telling me plainly what he was singing.' To this they laughed again and mocked him; but the one who had sung repeated the song to him, after which they went away laughing and singing.

' "Face," ' then said the poor belaboured

Peter as he got up slowly, 'will rhyme with "place"; now, Little Glass Man, I will have another word with you.' He went into the hut, took his hat and long stick, bade farewell to the inmates, and commenced his way back to the Tannenbühl. Being under the necessity of inventing a verse, he proceeded slowly and thoughtfully on his way; at length, when he was already within the precincts of the Tannenbühl, and the trees became higher and closer, he found his verse, and for joy cut a caper in the air. All at once he saw coming from behind the trees a gigantic man dressed like a raftsman, who held in his hand a pole as large as the mast of a ship. Peter Munk's knees almost gave way under him, when he saw him slowly striding by his side, thinking he was no other than the Dutchman Michel. Still the terrible figure kept silence, and Peter cast a side glance at him from time to time. He was full a head taller than the biggest man Peter had even seen; his face expressed neither youth nor old age, but was full of furrows and wrinkles; he wore a jacket of linen, and the enormous boots being drawn above his leather breeches, were well known to Peter from hearsay.

'What are you doing in the Tannenbühl, Peter Munk?' asked the wood king at length, in a deep, roaring voice.

'Good morning, countryman,' replied

Peter, wishing to show himself undaunted,
but trembling violently all the while.

'Peter Munk,' replied Michel, casting a
piercing, terrible glance at him, 'your way
does not lie through this grove.'

'True, it does not exactly,' said Peter,
'but being a hot day, I thought it would be
cooler here.'

'Do not lie, Peter,' cried Michel, in a
thundering voice, 'or I strike you to the
ground with this pole; think you I have not
seen you begging of the little one?' he
added mildly. 'Come, come, confess it was
a silly trick, and it is well you did not know
the verse; for the little fellow is a skinflint,
giving but little; and he to whom he gives
is never again cheerful in his life. Peter,
you are but a poor fool and I pity you in my
soul; you, such a brisk, handsome fellow,
surely could do something better in the
world than make charcoal. While others
lavish big thalers and ducats, you can
scarcely spend a few pence; 'tis a wretched
life.'

'You are right, it is truly a wretched life.'

'Well,' continued Michel, 'I will not
stand upon trifles; you would not be the
first honest good fellow whom I have
assisted at a pinch. Tell me, how many
hundred thalers do you want for the
present?' shaking the money in his huge
pocket, as he said this, so that it jingled

just as Peter had heard it in his dream.
But Peter's heart felt a kind of painful con-
vulsion at these words, and he was cold and
hot alternately; for Michel did not look as
if he would give away money out of charity,
without asking anything in return.   The
old man's mysterious words about rich
people occurred to him, and urged by an
inexplicable anxiety and fear, he cried,
'Much obliged to you, sir, but I will have
nothing to do with you and know you well,'
and at the same time he began to run as
fast as he could.   The wood spirit, however, strode by his side with immense
steps, murmuring and threatening, 'You
will repent it, Peter; it is written on your
forehead and to be read in your eyes that
you will not escape me.   Do not run so
fast, listen only to a single rational word;
there is my boundary already.'   But Peter,
hearing this and seeing at a little distance
before him a small ditch, hastened the more
to pass this boundary, so that Michel was
obliged at length to run faster, cursing and
threatening while pursuing him.   With a
desperate leap Peter cleared the ditch, for
he saw that the wood spirit was raising his
pole to dash it upon him; having fortunately
reached the other side, he heard the pole
shatter to pieces in the air as if against an
invisible wall, and a long piece fell down at
his feet.

He picked it up in triumph to throw it at the rude Michel; but in an instant he felt the piece of wood move in his hand, and, to his horror, perceived that he held an enormous serpent, which was raising itself up towards his face with its venomous tongue and glistening eyes. He let go his hold, but it had already twisted itself tight round his arm and came still closer to his face with its vibrating head; at this instant, however, an immense black cock rushed down, seized the head of the serpent with its beak, and carried it up in the air. Michel, who had observed all this from the other side of the ditch, howled, cried, and raved when he saw the serpent carried away by one more powerful than himself.

Exhausted and trembling, Peter continued his way; the path became steeper, the country wilder, and soon he found himself before the large pine. He again made a bow to the invisible Little Glass Man, as he had done the day before, and said—

'Keeper of wealth in the forest of pine,
Hundreds of years are surely thine,
Thine is the tall pine's dwelling place,
Those born on Sunday see thy face.'

'You have not quite hit it,' said a delicate fine voice near him, 'but as it is you, Peter, I will not be particular.' Astonished he looked round, and lo! under a beautiful pine there sat a little old man in a black jacket, red stockings, and a large hat on his head. He had a tiny affable face and a little beard as fine as a spider's web; and strange to see, he was smoking a pipe of blue glass. Nay, Peter observed to his astonishment, on coming nearer, that the clothes, shoes, and hat of the little man were also of coloured glass, which was as flexible as if it were still hot, bending like cloth to every motion of the little man.

'You have met the lubber Michel, the Dutchman?' asked the little man, laughing strangely between each word. 'He wished to frighten you terribly; but I have got his magic cudgel, which he shall never have again.'

'Yes, Mr. Schatzhauser,' replied Peter, with a profound bow, 'I was terribly frightened. But I suppose the black cock was yourself, and I am much obliged to you for killing the serpent. The object of my visit to you, however, is to ask your advice; I am in very poor circumstances, for charcoal-burning is not a profitable trade; and being still young I should think I might be made something better, seeing so often as I do how other people have thriven in a short time; I need only mention Hezekiel, and the king of the dancing-room, who have money like dirt.'

'Peter,' said the little man gravely, blowing the smoke of his pipe a long way off, 'don't talk to me of these men. What good have they from being apparently happy for a few years here, and the more unhappy for it afterwards? you must not despise your trade; your father and grandfather were honest people, Peter Munk, and they carried on the same trade. Let me not suppose it is love of idleness that brings you to me.'

Peter was startled at the gravity of the little man, and blushed. 'No, Mr. Schatzhauser,' said he; 'idleness is the root of every vice, but you cannot blame me, if another condition pleases me better than my own. A charcoal-burner is, in truth, a very mean personage in this world; the glass manufacturer, the raftsmen, and clockmakers, are people much more looked upon.'

'Pride will have a fall,' answered the little man of the pine wood, rather more kindly. 'What a singular race you are, you men! It is but rarely that one is contented with the condition in which he was born and bred, and I would lay a wager that if you were a glass manufacturer, you would wish to be a timber merchant, and if you were a timber merchant you would take a fancy to the ranger's place, or the residence of the bailiff. But no matter for that; if you promise to work hard, I will get you something better to do. It is my

practice to grant three wishes to those born
on a Sunday, who know how to find me
out.   The first two are quite free from any
condition, the third I may refuse, should it
be a foolish one.   Now, therefore, Peter,
say your wishes ; but mind you wish something good and useful.'

'Hurrah!' shouted Peter; 'you are a
capital glass man, and justly do people call
you the treasure-keeper, for treasures seem
to be plentiful with you.   Well, then, since
I may wish what my heart desires, my first
wish is that I may be able to dance better
than the king of the dancing-room, and to
have always as much money in my pocket
as fat Hezekiel.'

'You fool!' replied the little man
angrily, 'what a paltry wish is this, to be
able to dance well and to have money for
gambling.   Are you not ashamed of this
silly wish, you blockish Peter?   Would you
cheat yourself out of good fortune?   What
good will you and your poor mother reap
from your dancing well?   What use will
money be to you, which, according to your
wish, is only for the public-house, there to
be spent like that of the wretched king of
the dancing-room?   And then you will have
nothing for the whole week and starve.
Another wish is now left free to you; but
have a care to desire something more
rational.'

Peter scratched himself behind his ears, and said, after some hesitation, 'Now I wish for the finest and richest glass factory in the Schwarzwald, with everything appertaining to it, and money to carry it on.'

'Is that all?' asked the little man, with a look of anxiety; 'is there nothing else, Peter?'

'Why you might add a horse and chaise.'

'Oh, you stupid Peter!' cried the little man, while he flung his glass pipe against a thick pine so that it broke in a hundred pieces. 'Horses? a carriage? Sense, I tell you, sense—common sense and judgment you ought to have wished for, but not a horse and chaise. Come, come, don't be so sad, we will do all we can to make it turn out for the best, even as it is, for the second wish is on the whole not altogether foolish. A good glass factory will support its man; but you ought to have wished for judgment and sense in addition; a horse and chaise would come as a matter of course.'

'But, Mr. Schatzhauser,' replied Peter, 'I have another wish left, and might very well wish for sense, if I am so much in need of it, as you seem to think.'

'Say no more about it. You will get involved in many an embarrassment yet, when you will be glad of being at liberty to obtain your third wish. And now proceed on your way home.' Drawing a small bag from his pocket, he said : 'There are two thousand florins ; let that be enough, and don't come again asking for money, for, if you do, I must hang you up to the highest pine. That is the way I have always acted ever since I have lived in the forest. Three days ago old Winkfritz died, who had a large glass factory in the Unter-wald. Go there to-morrow morning, and make a fair offer for it. Look well to yourself. Be prudent and be industrious ; I will come to see you from time to time, and assist you with word and deed, since you have not wished for common sense. But I must repeat it seriously ; your first wish was evil. Guard against frequenting the public-house, Peter ; no one who did so ever prospered long.' The little man, while thus talking to him, had taken a new pipe, of the most beautiful glass, from his pocket, charged it with dry fir-apples, and stuck it into his little toothless mouth. Then drawing out a large burning - glass, he stepped into the sun and lighted it. When he had done this, he kindly offered his hand to Peter, added a few more words of salutary advice which he might carry on his way, puffed and blew still faster, and finally disappeared in a cloud of smoke, which smelled of genuine Dutch canaster, and, slowly curling upwards, vanished amidst the tops of the pines.

On his arrival home, Peter found his
mother in great anxiety about him, for the
good dame thought in reality her son had
been drawn among the recruits. He, however, was in great glee and full of hope, and
related to her how he had met with a good
friend in the forest, who had advanced him
money to begin another trade. Although
his mother had been living for thirty years
in a charcoal-burner's hut, and was as much
accustomed to the sight of sooty people
as any miller's wife is to the floury face of
her husband, yet, as soon as her Peter
showed her a more splendid lot, she was
vain enough to despise her former condition,
and said: 'In truth, as the mother of a
man who possesses a glass manufactory, I
shall indeed be something different from
neighbour Kate and Betsy, and shall in
future sit more consequentially at church
among the people of quality.' Her son
soon came to terms with the heir of the
glass manufactory. He kept the workmen
he found, and made them work day and night
at manufacturing glass. At first he was
pleased well enough with his new trade; he
was in the habit of walking leisurely into the
factory, striding up and down with an air
of consequence and with his hands in his
pockets, looking now in one corner, now in
another, and talking about various things at
which his workmen often used to laugh

heartily. His chief delight, however, was to see the glass blown, when he would often set to work himself, and form the strangest figures of the soft mass. But he soon took a dislike to the work; first he came only for an hour in the day, then only every other day, and finally only once a week, so that his workmen did just what they liked. All this came from his frequenting the public-house. The Sunday after he had come back from the Tannenbühl he went to the public-house, and who should be jumping there already but the king of the dancing-room; fat Hezekiel also was already sitting by a quart pot, playing at dice for crown-pieces. Now Peter quickly put his hand into his pocket to feel whether the Little Glass Man had been true to his word, and lo! his pockets were stuffed full of silver and gold. He also felt an itching and twitching in his legs, as if they wished to dance and caper. When the first dance was over, he took his place with his partner at the top next to the king of the dancing-room; and if the latter jumped three feet high, Peter jumped four; if he made fantastic and graceful steps, Peter twined and twisted his legs in such a manner that all the spectators were utterly amazed with delight and admiration. But when it was rumoured in the dancing-room that Peter had bought a glass manufactory, and when people saw that Peter, as often as he passed the musicians, threw a six-bätzner piece to them, there was no end of astonishment. Some thought he had found a treasure in the forest, others were of opinion that he had succeeded to some fortune, but all respected him now, and considered him a made man, simply because he had plenty of money. Indeed that very evening he lost twenty florins at play, and yet his pockets jingled and tingled as if there were a hundred thalers in them.

When Peter saw how much respected he was, he could no longer contain himself with joy and pride. He threw away handfuls of money and distributed it profusely among the poor, knowing full well as he did how poverty had formerly pinched him. The feats of the king of the dancing-room were completely eclipsed by those of the new dancer, and Peter was surnamed the 'emperor of the dancing - room.' The most daring gamblers did not stake so much as he did on a Sunday, neither did they, however, lose so much; but then, the more he lost, the more he won. This was exactly what he had demanded from the Little Glass Man; for he had wished he might always have as much money in his pocket as fat Hezekiel, and it was to this very man he lost his money. If he lost twenty or thirty florins at a stroke, they were immediately

replaced in his own pocket, as soon as
Hezekiel pocketed them. By degrees he
carried his revelling and gambling further
than the worst fellows in the Schwarzwald,
and he was oftener called 'gambling Peter'
than 'emperor of the dancing-room,' since
he now gambled almost all days of the week.
In consequence of his imprudence, his glass
manufactory gradually fell off. He had
manufactured as much as ever could be
made, but he had failed to purchase, together
with the factory, the secret of disposing of it
most profitably. At length it accumulated
to such a degree that he did not know what
to do with it, and sold it for half price to
itinerant dealers in order to pay his workmen.

Walking homewards one evening from the
public-house, he could not, in spite of the
quantity of wine he had drunk to make himself merry, help thinking with terror and
grief of the decline of his fortune. While
engaged in these reflections, he all at once
perceived some one walking by his side. He
looked round, and behold it was the Little
Glass Man. At the sight of him he fell into
a violent passion, protested solemnly, and
swore that the little man was the cause of
all his misfortune. 'What am I to do now
with the horse and chaise?' he cried; 'of
what use is the manufactory and all the glass
to me? Even when I was merely a wretched

charcoal-burner, I lived more happily, and had no cares. Now I know not when the bailiff may come to value my goods and chattels, and seize all for debt.'

'Indeed?' replied the Little Glass Man, 'indeed?   I am then the cause of your being unfortunate. Is that your gratitude for my benefits? Who bade you wish so foolishly? A glass manufacturer you wished to be, and you did not know where to sell your glass! Did I not tell you to be cautious in what you wished for? Common sense, Peter, and prudence, you wanted.'

'A fig for your sense and prudence,' cried Peter ; 'I am as shrewd a fellow as any one, and will prove it to you, Little Glass Man,' seizing him rudely by the collar as he spoke these words, and crying, 'Have I now got you, Schatzhauser? Now I will tell you my third wish, which you shall grant me. I'll have instantly, on the spot, two hundred thousand hard thalers and a house. Woe is me !' he cried, suddenly shaking his hand, for the little man of the wood had changed himself into red-hot glass, and burned in his hand like bright fire. Nothing more was to be seen of him.

For several days his swollen hand re-minded him of his ingratitude and folly. Soon, however, he silenced his conscience, saying : 'Should they sell my glass, manu-factory and all, still fat Hezekiel is certain

E

to me; and as long as he has money on a Sunday, I cannot want.'

'Very true, Peter!   But, if he has none?' And so it happened one day, and it proved a singular example in arithmetic.   For he came one Sunday in his chaise to the inn, and at once all the people popped their heads out of the windows, one saying, 'There comes gambling Peter;' a second saying, 'Yes, there is the emperor of the dancing-room, the wealthy glass manufacturer;' while a third shook his head, saying, 'It is all very well with his wealth, but people talk a great deal about his debts, and somebody in town has said that the bailiff will not wait much longer before he distrains upon him.'

At this moment the wealthy Peter saluted the guests at the windows in a haughty and grave manner, descended from his chaise, and cried : 'Good evening, mine Host of the Sun.   Is fat Hezekiel here?'

To this question a deep voice answered from within : 'Only come in, Peter; your place is kept for you; we are all here at the cards already.'

Peter entering the parlour, immediately put his hand into his pocket, and perceived, by its being quite full, that Hezekiel must be plentifully supplied.   He sat down at the table among the others and played, losing and winning alternately; thus they kept playing till night, when all sober people went home. After having continued for some time by candle-light, two of the gamblers said : 'Now it is enough, and we must go home to our wives and children.'

But Peter challenged Hezekiel to remain. The latter was unwilling, but said, after a while, 'Be it as you wish ; I will count my money, and then we'll play dice at five florins the stake, for anything lower is, after all, but child's play.' He drew his purse, and, after counting, found he had a hundred florins left ; now Peter knew how much he himself had left, without counting first. But if Hezekiel had won before, he now lost stake after stake, and swore most awfully. If he cast a *pasch*, Peter immediately cast one likewise, and always two points higher. At length he put down the last five florins on the table, saying, 'Once more ; and if I lose this stake also, yet I will not leave off ; you will then lend me some of the money you have won now, Peter ; one honest fellow helps the other.'

'As much as you like, even if it were a hundred florins,' replied Peter, joyful at his gain, and fat Hezekiel rattled the dice and threw up fifteen ; 'Pasch !' he exclaimed, 'now we'll see !' But Peter threw up eighteen, and, at this moment, a hoarse, well-known voice said behind him, 'So! that was the last.'

He looked round, and behind him stood

the gigantic figure of Michel the Dutchman. Terrified, he dropped the money he had already taken up. But fat Hezekiel, not seeing Michel, demanded that Peter should advance him ten florins for playing. As if in a dream, Peter hastily put his hand into his pocket, but there was no money; he searched in the other pocket, but in vain; he turned his coat inside out, not a farthing, however, fell out; and at this instant he first recollected his first wish, viz. to have always as much money in his pocket as fat Hezekiel. All had now vanished like smoke.

The host and Hezekiel looked at him with astonishment as he still searched for and could not find his money; they would not believe that he had no more left; but when they at length searched his pockets, without finding anything, they were enraged, swearing that gambling Peter was an evil wizard, and had wished away all the money he had won home to his own house. Peter defended himself stoutly, but appearances were against him. Hezekiel protested he would tell this shocking story to all the people in the Schwarzwald, and the host vowed he would the following morning early go into the town and inform against Peter as a sorcerer, adding that he had no doubt of his being burnt alive. Upon this they fell furiously upon him, tore off his coat, and kicked him out of doors.

Not one star was twinkling in the sky to

lighten Peter's way as he sneaked sadly towards his home, but still he could distinctly recognise a dark form striding by his side, which at length said, ' It is all over with you, Peter Munk ; all your splendour is at an end, and this I could have foretold you even at the time when you would not listen to me, but rather ran to the silly glass dwarf. You now see to what you have come by disregarding my advice. But try your fortune with me this time, I have compassion on your fate. No one ever yet repented of applying to me, and if you don't mind the walk to the Tannenbühl, I shall be there all day to-morrow and you may speak to me, if you will call.' Peter now very clearly perceived who was speaking to him, but feeling a sensation of awe, he made no answer and ran towards home.

When, on the Monday morning, he came to his factory, he not only found his workmen, but also other people whom no one likes to see, viz. the bailiff and three beadles. The bailiff wished Peter good morning, asked him how he had slept, and then took from his pocket a long list of Peter's creditors, saying, with a stern look, ' Can you pay or not ? Be short, for I have no time to lose, and you know it is full three leagues to the prison.' Peter in despair confessed he had nothing left, telling the bailiff he might value all the premises, horses and

carts. But while they went about examining
and valuing the things, Peter said to himself, 'Well, it is but a short way to the
Tannenbühl, and as the *little* man has not
helped me, I will now for once try the *big*
man.' He ran towards the Tannenbühl as
fast as if the beadles were at his heels. On
passing the spot where the Little Glass Man
had first spoken to him, he felt as if an
invisible hand were stopping him, but he
tore himself away, and ran onwards till he
came to the boundary which he had well
marked. Scarcely had he, quite out of
breath, called 'Dutch Michel, Mr. Dutch
Michel!' when suddenly the gigantic raftsman with his pole stood before him.

'Have you come then?' said the latter,
laughing. 'Were they going to fleece you
and sell you to your creditors? Well, be
easy, all your sorrow comes, as I have always
said, from the Little Glass Man, the Separa-
tist and Pietist. When one gives, one ought
to give right plentifully and not like that
skinflint. But come,' he continued, turning
towards the forest, 'follow me to my house,
there we'll see whether we can strike a
bargain.'

'Strike a bargain?' thought Peter.
'What can he want of me, what can I sell to
him? Am I perhaps to serve him, or what
is it that he can want?' They went at first
uphill over a steep forest path, when all at

once they stopped at a dark, deep, and almost perpendicular ravine. Michel leaped down as easily as he would go down marble steps ; but Peter almost fell into a fit when he saw him below, rising up like a church steeple, reaching him an arm as long as a scaffolding pole, with a hand at the end as broad as the table in the ale-house, and calling in a voice which sounded like the deep tones of a death bell, 'Set yourself boldly on my hand, hold fast by the fingers and you will not fall off.' Peter, trembling, did as he was ordered, sat down upon his hand and held himself fast by the thumb of the giant.

They now went down a long way and very deep, yet, to Peter's astonishment, it did not grow darker ; on the contrary, the daylight seemed rather to increase in the chasm, and it was some time before Peter's eyes could bear it. Michel's stature became smaller as Peter came lower down, and he stood now in his former size before a house just like those of the wealthy peasants of the Schwarzwald. The room into which Peter was led differed in nothing but its appearance of solitariness from those of other people. The wooden clock, the stove of Dutch tiles, the broad benches and utensils on the shelves were the same as anywhere else. Michel told him to sit down at the large table, then went out of the room and returned with a pitcher of wine and glasses. Having filled these, they now began a conversation, and Dutch Michel expatiated on the pleasures of the world, talked of foreign countries, fine cities and rivers, so that Peter, at length, feeling a yearning after such sights, candidly told Michel his wish.

' If you had courage and strength in your body to undertake anything, could a few palpitations of your stupid heart make you tremble ; and the offences against honour, or misfortunes, why should a rational fellow care for either ? Did you feel it in your head when they but lately called you a cheat and a scoundrel ? Or did it give you a pain in your stomach, when the bailiff came to eject you from your house ? Tell me, where was it you felt pain ? '

' In my heart,' replied Peter, putting his hand on his beating breast, for he felt as if his heart was anxiously turning within him.

' Excuse me for saying so, but you have thrown away many hundred florins on vile beggars and other rabble ; what has it pro-fited you ? They have wished you blessings and health for it ; well, have you grown the healthier for that ? For half that money you might have kept a physician. A bless-ing, a fine blessing, forsooth, when one is distrained upon and ejected ! And what was it that urged you put your hand into your pocket, as often as a beggar held out his broken hat?—Why your heart again, and ever your heart, neither your eyes, nor your tongue, nor your arms, nor your legs, but your heart; you have, as the proverb truly says, taken too much to heart.'

'But how can we accustom ourselves to act otherwise? I take, at this moment, every possible pains to suppress it, and yet my heart palpitates and pains me.'

'You, indeed, poor fellow!' cried Michel, laughing; 'you can do nothing against it; but give me this scarcely palpitating thing, and you will see how comfortable you will then feel.'

'My heart to you?' cried Peter, horrified. 'Why, then, I must die on the spot! Never!'

'Yes, if one of your surgeons would operate upon you and take out your heart, you must indeed die; but with me it is a different thing; just come in here and convince yourself.'

Rising at these words, he opened the door of a chamber and took Peter in. On stepping over the threshold, his heart contracted convulsively, but he minded it not, for the sight that presented itself was singular and surprising. On several shelves glasses were standing, filled with a transparent liquid, and each contained a heart. All were labelled with names which Peter read with curiosity; there was the heart of the bailiff in F., that of fat Hezekiel, that of the king of the dancing-room, that of the ranger; there were the hearts of six usurious corn merchants, of eight recruiting officers, of three money-brokers; in short, it was a collection of the most respectable hearts twenty leagues around.

'Look!' said Dutch Michel, 'all these have shaken off the anxieties and cares of life; none of these hearts any longer beat anxiously and uneasily, and their former owners feel happy now they have got rid of the troublesome guest.'

'But what do they now carry in their breasts instead?' asked Peter, whose head was nearly swimming at what he beheld.

'*This*,' replied he, taking out of a small drawer, and presenting to him—a heart of stone.

'Indeed!' said Peter, who could not prevent a cold shuddering coming over him. 'A heart of marble? But, tell me, Mr. Michel, such a heart must be very cold in one's breast.'

'True, but very agreeably cool. Why should a heart be warm? For in winter its warmth is of little use, and good strong Kirschwasser does more than a warm heart, and in summer when all is hot and sultry, you can't think how cooling such a heart is. And, as before said, such a heart feels neither

THE LITTLE GLASS MAN

anxiety nor terror, neither foolish compassion nor other grief.'

'And that is all you can offer me?' asked Peter indignantly; 'I looked for money and you are going to give me a stone.'

'Well! an hundred thousand florins, methinks, would suffice you for the present. If you employ it properly, you may soon make it a million.'

'An hundred thousand!' exclaimed the poor coal-burner, joyfully. 'Well, don't beat so vehemently in my bosom, we shall soon have done with one another. Agreed, Michel, give me the stone and the money, and the alarum you may take out of its case.'

'I always thought you were a reasonable fellow,' replied Michel, with a friendly smile; 'come, let us drink another glass, and then I will pay you the money.'

They went back to the room and sat down again to the wine, drinking one glass after another till Peter fell into a profound sleep.

He was awakened by the cheerful blast of a post-boy's bugle, and found himself sitting in a handsome carriage, driving along on a wide road. On putting his head out he saw in the airy distance the Schwarzwald lying behind him. At first he could scarcely believe that it was his own self sitting in the carriage, for even his clothes were different from those he had worn the day before; but still he had such a distinct recollection that, giving up at length all these reflections, he exclaimed, ' I am Peter and no other, that is certain.'

He was astonished that he could not, in the slightest degree, feel melancholy now that he for the first time departed from his quiet home and the forests where he had lived so long. He could not even press a tear out of his eyes or utter a sigh, when he thought of his mother, who must now feel helpless and wretched ; for he was indifferent to everything : 'Well,' he said, 'tears and sighs, yearning for home and sadness, proceed indeed from the heart, but thanks to Dutch Michel, mine is of stone and cold.' Putting his hand upon his breast, he felt all quiet and no emotion. 'If Michel,' said he, beginning to search the carriage, 'keeps his word as well with respect to the hundred thousand florins as he does with the heart, I shall be very glad.' In his search he found articles of dress of every description he could wish, but no money. At length, however, he discovered a pocket containing many thousand thalers in gold, and bills on large houses in all the great cities. 'Now I have what I want,' thought he, squeezed himself into the corner of the carriage and went into the wide world.

For two years he travelled about in the world, looked from his carriage to the right and left up the houses, but whenever he alighted he looked at nothing except the sign of the hotel, and then ran about the town to see the finest curiosities. But nothing gladdened him, no pictures, no building, no music, no dancing, nor anything else had any interest for, or excited his stone heart; his eyes and ears were blunted for everything beautiful. No enjoyment was left him but that which he felt in eating and drinking and sleep; and thus he lived running through the world without any object, eating for amusement and sleeping from *ennui*. From time to time he indeed remembered that he had been more cheerful and happier, when he was poor and obliged to work for a livelihood. Then he was delighted by every beautiful prospect in the valley, by music and song, then he had for hours looked in joyful expectation towards the frugal meal which his mother was to bring him to the kiln.

When thus reflecting on the past, it seemed very strange to him that now he could not even laugh, while formerly he had laughed at the slightest joke. When others laughed, he only distorted his mouth out of politeness, but his heart did not sympathise with the smile. He felt he was indeed exceedingly tranquil, but yet not contented. It was not a yearning after home, nor was it sadness, but a void, desolate feeling, satiety and a joyless life that at last urged him to his home.

When, after leaving Strasburg, he beheld
the dark forest of his native country ; when
for the first time he again saw the robust
figures, the friendly and open countenances
of the Schwarzwälder ; when the homely,
strong, and deep, but harmonious sounds
struck upon his ear, he quickly put his hand
upon his heart, for his blood flowed faster,
thinking he must rejoice and weep at the
same time ; but how could he be so foolish ?
he had a heart of stone, and stones are dead
and can neither smile nor weep.

His first walk was to Michel, who received
him with his former kindness. ' Michel,'
said he, ' I have now travelled and seen
everything, but all is dull stuff and I have
only found *ennui*.   The stone I carry about
with me in my breast, protects me against
many things ; I never get angry, am never
sad, but neither do I ever feel joyful, and it
seems as if I were only half alive.   Can you
not infuse a little more life into my stone
heart, or rather, give me back my former
heart ?   During five-and-twenty years I had
become quite accustomed to it, and though
it sometimes did a foolish thing, yet it was,
after all, a merry and cheerful heart.'

The sylvan spirit laughed grimly and sar-
castically at this, answering, ' When once
you are dead, Peter Munk, it shall not be
withheld ; then you shall have back your
soft, susceptible heart, and may then feel

whatever comes, whether joy or sorrow. But here, on this side of the grave, it can never be yours again. Travelled you have indeed, Peter, but in the way you lived, your travelling could afford you no satisfaction. Settle now somewhere in the world, build a house, marry, and employ your capital ; you wanted nothing but occupation ; being idle, you felt *ennui*, and now you lay all the blame on this innocent heart.' Peter saw that Michel was right with respect to idleness, and therefore proposed to himself to become richer and richer. Michel gave him another hundred thousand florins, and they parted good friends.

The report soon spread in the Schwarzwald that 'Coal Peter,' or 'gambling Peter,' had returned, and was much richer than before. It was here as it is always. When he was a beggar he was kicked out of the inn, but now he had come back wealthy, all shook him by the hand when he entered on the Sunday afternoon, praised his horse, asked about his journey, and when he began playing for hard dollars with fat Hezekiel, he stood as high in their estimation as ever before. He no longer followed the trade of glass manufacturer, but the timber trade, though that only in appearance, his chief business being in corn and money trans-actions. Half the people of the Schwarzwald became by degrees his debtors, and he lent

money only at 10 per cent, or sold corn to
the poor, who, not being able to pay ready
money, had to purchase it at three times its
value.   With the bailiff he now stood on a
footing of the closest friendship, and if any
one failed paying Mr. Peter Munk on the
very day the money was due, the bailiff with
his beadles came, valued house and property,
sold all instantly, and drove father, mother,
and child out into the forest.   This became
at first rather troublesome to Peter, for the
poor outcasts besieged his doors in troops,
the men imploring indulgence, the women
trying to move his stony heart, and the
children moaning for a piece of bread.   But
getting a couple of large mastiffs, he soon
put an end to this cat's music, as he used to
call it, for he whistled and set them on the
beggars, who dispersed screaming.   But the
most troublesome person to him was 'the
old woman,' who, however, was no other
than Frau Munk, Peter's mother.   She had
been reduced to great poverty and distress,
when her house and all was sold, and her
son, on returning wealthy, had troubled
himself no more about her.   So she came
sometimes before his house, supporting herself on a stick, as she was aged, weak, and
infirm ; but she no more ventured to go in,
as he had on one occasion driven her out ;
and she was much grieved at being obliged
to prolong her existence by the bounties of

other people, while her own son might have prepared for her a comfortable old age. But his cold heart never was moved by the sight of the pale face and well-known features, by her imploring looks, outstretched withered hands, and decaying frame. If on a Saturday she knocked at the door, he put his hand grumbling into his pocket for a six-batzen piece, wrapped it in a bit of paper, and sent it out by a servant. He heard her tremulous voice when she thanked him, and wished him a blessing in this world, he heard her crawl away coughing from the door, but he thought of nothing except that he had again spent six batzen for nothing.

At length Peter took it into his head to marry. He knew that every father in the Schwarzwald would gladly give him his daughter, but he was fastidious in his choice, for he wished that everybody should praise his good fortune and understanding in matrimony as well as in other matters. He therefore rode about the whole forest, looking out in every direction, but none of the pretty Schwarzwälder girls seemed beautiful enough for him. Having finally looked out in vain for the most beautiful at all the dancing-rooms, he was one day told the most beautiful and most virtuous girl in the whole forest was the daughter of a poor wood-cutter. He heard she lived quiet and retired, was industrious and managed her

F

father's household well, and that she was
never seen at a dancing-room, not even at
Whitsuntide or the Kirchweihfest.[1]   When
Peter heard of this wonder of the Schwarzwald, he determined to court her, and,
having inquired where the hut was, rode
there.   The father· of the beautiful Elizabeth received the great gentleman with
astonishment, but was still more amazed
when he heard it was the rich Herr Peter
who wished to become his son-in-law.
Thinking all his cares and poverty would
now be at an end, he did not hesitate long
in giving his consent, without even asking
the beautiful Elizabeth, and the good child
was so dutiful that she became Frau Peter
Munk without opposition.

But the poor girl did not find the happiness she had dreamt of.   She believed she
understood the management of a house well,
but she could never give satisfaction to Herr
Peter ; she had compassion on poor people,
and, as her husband was wealthy, thought it
no sin to give a poor woman a penny, or a
dram to a poor aged man.   This being one
day found out by Peter, he said to her, with
angry look and gruff voice, 'Why do you
waste my property upon ragamuffins and
vagabonds ?   Have you brought anything of
your own to the house that you can give

[1] A great festival in German villages, which comes
in October or November.

away? With your father's beggar's staff you could not warm a soup, and you lavish my money like a princess. Once more let me find you out, and you shall feel my hand.' The beautiful Elizabeth wept in her chamber over the hard heart of her husband, and often wished herself at home in her father's poor hut rather than with the rich, but avaricious and sinful Peter. Alas! had she known that he had a heart of marble and could neither love her nor anybody else, she would not, perhaps, have wondered. But as often as a beggar now passed while she was sitting before the door, and drawing his hat off, asked for alms, she shut her eyes that she might not behold his distress, and closed her hand tight that she might not put it involuntarily in her pocket and take out a kreutzer. This caused a report and obtained an ill name for Elizabeth in the whole forest, and she was said to be even more miserly than Peter Munk. But one day Frau Elizabeth was again sitting before the door spinning and humming an air, for she was cheerful because it was fine weather, and Peter was taking a ride in the country, when a little old man came along the road, carrying a large heavy bag, and she heard him panting at a great distance. Sympathisingly she looked at him and thought how cruel it was to place such a heavy burden upon an aged man.

In the meanwhile the little man came near, tottering and panting, and sank under the weight of his bag almost down on the ground just as he came opposite Frau Elizabeth.

' Oh, have compassion on me, good woman, and give me a drink of water,' said the little man ; ' I can go no farther, and must perish from exhaustion.'

' But you ought not to carry such heavy loads at your age,' said she.

' No more I should if I were not obliged to work as carrier from poverty and to prolong my life,' replied he. ' Ah, such rich ladies as you know not how painful poverty is, and how strengthening a fresh draught would be in this hot weather.'

On hearing this she immediately ran into the house, took a pitcher from the shelf and filled it with water ; but she had only gone a few paces back to take it to him, when, seeing the little man sit on his bag miserable and wretched, she felt pity for him, and recollecting that her husband was from home, she put down the pitcher, took a cup, filled it with wine, put a loaf of rye bread on it, and gave it to the poor old man. ' There,' she said, ' a draught of wine will do you more good than water, as you are very old ; but do not drink so hastily, and eat some bread with it.'

The little man looked at her in astonishment till the big tears came into his eyes; he drank and said, 'I have grown old, but have seen few people who were so compassionate and knew how to spend their gifts so handsomely and cordially as you do, Frau Elizabeth. But you will be blessed for it on earth; such a heart will not remain unrequited.'

'No, and she shall have her reward on the spot,' cried a terrible voice, and looking round they found it was Herr Peter, with a face as red as scarlet. 'Even my choicest wine you waste upon beggars, and give my own cup to the lips of vagabonds? There, take your reward.' His wife fell prostrate before him and begged his forgiveness, but the heart of stone knew no pity, and flourishing the whip he held in his hand, he struck her with the ebony handle on her beautiful forehead with such vehemence that she sank lifeless into the arms of the old man. When he saw what he had done it was almost as if he repented of the deed immediately; he stooped to see whether there was yet life in her, but the little man said in a well-known voice, 'Spare your trouble, Peter; she was the most beautiful and lovely flower in the Schwarzwald, but you have crushed it and never again will see it bloom.'

Now the blood fled from Peter's cheek and he said, 'It is you, then, Mr. Schatzhauser? well, what is done is done then, and I suppose this was to happen. But I trust you will not inform against me.'

'Wretch,' replied the Little Glass Man, 'what would it profit me if I brought your mortal part to the gallows? It is not earthly tribunals you have to fear, but another and more severe one; for you have sold your soul to the evil one.'

'And if I have sold my heart,' cried Peter, 'it is no one's fault but yours and your deceitful treasures'; your malicious spirit brought me to ruin; you forced me to seek help from another, and upon you lies the whole responsibility.' He had scarcely uttered these words when the little man grew enormously tall and broad, his eyes it is said became as large as soup plates, and his mouth like a heated furnace vomiting flames. Peter fell upon his knees, and his stone heart did not protect his limbs from trembling like an aspen leaf. The sylvan spirit seized him, as if with vultures' claws, by the nape of the neck, whirled him round as the storm whirls the dry leaves, and dashed him to the ground so that his ribs cracked within him. 'You worm of dust,' he cried, in a voice roaring like thunder, 'I could crush you if I wished, for you have trespassed against the lord of the forest; but for the sake of this dead woman that fed and refreshed me, I give you a week's respite. If you do not repent I shall return and crush your bones, and you will go hence in your sins.'

It was already evening when some men passing by saw the wealthy Peter Munk lying on the ground. They turned him over and over to see whether there was still life in him, but for a long time looked in vain. At length one of them went into the house, fetched some water and sprinkled some on his face. Peter fetched a deep sigh and opened his eyes, looked for a long time around, and asked for his wife Elizabeth, but no one had seen her. He thanked the men for their assistance, crawled into his house, searched everywhere, but in vain, and found what he imagined to be a dream a sad reality. As he was now quite alone strange thoughts came into his mind; he did not indeed fear anything, for his heart was quite cold; but when he thought of the death of his wife his own forcibly came to his mind, and he reflected how laden he should go hence—heavily laden with the tears of the poor; with thousands of the curses of those who could not soften his heart; with the lamentations of the wretched on whom he had set his dogs; with the silent despair of his mother; with the blood of the beautiful and good Elizabeth; and yet he could not even so much as give an account of her to her poor old father, should he come and ask, 'Where is my daughter, your wife?' How then could he give an account to Him—to Him to whom belong all woods, all lakes, all mountains, and the life of men?

This tormented him in his dreams at night, and he was awoke every moment by a sweet voice crying to him, 'Peter, get a warmer heart!' And when he was awoke he quickly closed his eyes again, for the voice uttering this warning to him could be none other but that of his Elizabeth. The following day he went into the inn to divert his thoughts, and there met his friend, fat Hezekiel. He sat down by him and they commenced talking on various topics, of the fine weather, of war, of taxes, and lastly, also of death, and how such and such a person had died suddenly. Now Peter asked him what he thought about death, and how it would be after death. Hezekiel replied, 'That the body was buried, but that the soul went either up to heaven or down to hell.'

'Then the heart also is buried?' asked Peter, anxiously.

'To be sure that also is buried.'

'But supposing one has no longer a heart?' continued Peter.

Hezekiel gave him a terrible look at these words. 'What do you mean by that? Do you wish to rally me? Think you I have no heart?'

'Oh, heart enough, as firm as stone,' replied Peter.

Hezekiel looked in astonishment at him, glancing round at the same time to see whether they were overheard, and then said, ' Whence do you know that ?   Or does your own perhaps no longer beat within your breast ? '

' It beats no longer, at least, not in my breast,' replied Peter Munk.   ' But tell me, as you know what I mean, how will it be with our hearts ? '

' Why does that concern you, my good fellow ? ' answered Hezekiel, laughing. ' Why, you have plenty here upon earth, and that is sufficient.   Indeed, the comfort of our cold hearts is that no fear at such thoughts befalls us.'

' Very true, but still one cannot help thinking of it, and though I know no fear now, still I well remember how I was terrified at hell when yet an innocent little boy.'

' Well, it will not exactly go well with us,' said Hezekiel ; ' I once asked a schoolmaster about it, who told me that the hearts are weighed after death to ascertain the weight of their sins.   The light ones rise, the heavy sink, and methinks our stone hearts will weigh heavy enough.'

' Alas, true,' replied Peter ; ' I often feel uncomfortable that my heart is so devoid of sympathy, and so indifferent when I think of such things.'   So ended their conversation.

But the following night Peter again heard

the well-known voice whispering into his ear five or six times, 'Peter, get a warmer heart!' He felt no repentance at having killed his wife, but when he told the servants that she had gone on a journey, he always thought within himself, where is she gone to? Six days had thus passed away, and he still heard the voice at night, and still thought of the sylvan spirit and his terrible menace; but on the seventh morning he jumped up from his couch and cried, 'Well, then, I will see whether I can get a warmer heart, for the cold stone in my breast makes my life only tedious and desolate.' He quickly put on his best dress, mounted his horse, and rode towards the Tannenbühl.

Having arrived at that part where the trees stand thickest, he dismounted, and went with a quick pace towards the summit of the hill, and as he stood before the thick pine he repeated the following verse:

> ' Keeper of wealth in the forest of pine,
> Hundreds of years are surely thine :
> Thine is the tall pine's dwelling-place—
> Those born on Sunday see thy face.'

The Little Glass Man appeared, not looking friendly and kindly as formerly, but gloomy and sad; he wore a little coat of black glass, and a long glass crape hung floating from his hat, and Peter well knew for whom he mourned.

'What do you want with me, Peter Munk?'
asked he with a stern voice.

'I have one more wish, Mr. Schatzhauser,'
replied Peter, with his eyes cast down.

'Can hearts of stone still wish?' said the
former. 'You have all your corrupt mind
can need, and I could scarcely fulfil your
wish.'

'But you have promised to grant me
three wishes, and one I have still left.'

'I can refuse it if it is foolish,' continued
the spirit; 'but come, let me hear what you
wish.'

'Well, take the dead stone out of me, and
give me a living heart,' said Peter.

'Have I made the bargain about the heart
with you?' asked the Little Glass Man.
'Am I the Dutch Michel, who gives wealth
and cold hearts? It is of him you must
seek to regain your heart.'

'Alas! he will never give it back,' said
Peter.

'Bad as you are, yet I feel pity for you,'
continued the little man, after some consideration; 'and as your wish is not foolish,
I cannot at least refuse my help. Hear
then. You can never recover your heart by
force, only by stratagem, but probably you
will find it without difficulty; for Michel will
ever be stupid Michel, although he fancies
himself very shrewd. Go straightway to
him, and do as I tell you.' He now in-

structed Peter fully, and gave him a small cross of pure glass, saying, 'He cannot touch your life and will let you go when you hold this before him and repeat a prayer. When you have obtained your wish return to me.'

Peter took the cross, impressed all the words on his memory, and started on his way to the Dutchman Michel's residence; there he called his name three times and immediately the giant stood before him.

'You have slain your wife?' he asked, with a grim laugh. 'I should have done the same; she wasted your property on beggars; but you will be obliged to leave the country for some time; and I suppose you want money and have come to get it?'

'You have hit it,' replied Peter; 'and pray let it be a large sum, for it is a long way to America.'

Michel leading the way, they went into his cottage; there he opened a chest containing much money and took out whole rolls of gold. While he was counting it on the table Peter said, 'You're a wag, Michel. You have told me a fib, saying that I had a stone in my breast, and that you had my heart.'

'And is it not so then?' asked Michel, astonished. 'Do you feel your heart? Is it not cold as ice? Have you any fear or sorrow? Do you repent of anything?'

'You have only made my heart to cease beating, but I still have it in my breast, and so has Hezekiel, who told me you had deceived us both. You are not the man who, unperceived and without danger, could tear the heart from the breast; it would require witchcraft on your part.'

'But I assure you,' cried Michel angrily, 'you and Hezekiel and all the rich people, who have sold themselves to me, have hearts as cold as yours, and their real hearts I have here in my chamber.'

'Ah! how glibly you can tell lies,' said Peter, laughing; 'you must tell that to another to be believed; think you I have not seen such tricks by dozens in my journeys? Your hearts in the chamber are made of wax; you're a rich fellow I grant, but you are no magician.'

Now the giant was enraged and burst open the chamber door, saying, 'Come in and read all the labels, and look yonder is Peter Munk's heart; do you see how it writhes? Can that too be of wax?'

'For all that, it is of wax,' replied Peter. 'A genuine heart does not writhe like that. I have mine still in my breast. No! you are no magician.'

'But I will prove it to you,' cried the former angrily. 'You shall feel that it is your heart.' He took it, opened Peter's waistcoat, took the stone from his breast, and held it up. Then taking the heart, he breathed on it, and set it carefully in its proper place, and immediately Peter felt how it beat, and could rejoice again. 'How do you feel now?' asked Michel, smiling.

'True enough, you were right,' replied Peter, taking carefully the little cross from his pocket. 'I should never have believed such things could be done.'

'You see I know something of witchcraft, do I not? But, come, I will now replace the stone again.'

'Gently, Herr Michel,' cried Peter, stepping backwards, and holding up the cross, 'mice are caught with bacon, and this time you have been deceived,' and immediately he began to repeat the prayers that came into his mind.

Now Michel became less and less, fell to the ground, and writhed like a worm, groaning and moaning, and all the hearts round began to beat, and became convulsed, so hat it sounded like a clock-maker's workshop.

Peter was terrified, his mind was quite disturbed; he ran from the house, and, urged by the anguish of the moment, climbed up a steep rock, for he heard Michel get up, stamping and raving, and denouncing curses on him. When he reached the top, he ran towards the Tannenbühl; a dreadful thunderstorm came on; lightning flashed around him, splitting the trees, but he reached the precincts of the Little Glass Man in safety.

His heart beat joyfully—only because it *did* beat; but now he looked back with horror on his past life, as he did on the thunderstorm that was destroying the beautiful forest on his right and left. He thought of his wife, a beautiful, good woman, whom he had murdered from avarice; he appeared to himself an outcast from mankind, and wept bitterly as he reached the hill of the Little Glass Man.

The Schatzhauser was sitting under a pine-tree, and was smoking a small pipe; but he looked more serene than before.

'Why do you weep, Peter?' asked he; 'have you not recovered your heart? Is the cold one still in your breast?'

'Alas! sir,' sighed Peter, 'when I still carried about with me the cold stony heart, I never wept, my eyes were as dry as the ground in July; but now my old heart will almost break with what I have done. I have driven my debtors to misery, set the dogs on the sick and poor, and you yourself know how my whip fell upon *her* beautiful forehead.'

'Peter, you were a great sinner,' said the little man. 'Money and idleness corrupted you, until your heart turned to stone, and no longer knew joy, sorrow, repentance, or compassion. But repentance reconciles;

and if I only knew that you were truly sorry for your past life, it might yet be in my power to do something for you.'

'I wish nothing more,' replied Peter, dropping his head sorrowfully. 'It is all over with me, I can no more rejoice in my lifetime ; what shall I do thus alone in the world ? My mother will never pardon me for what I have done to her, and I have perhaps brought her to the grave, monster that I am ! Elizabeth, my wife, too,— rather strike me dead, Herr Schatzhauser, then my wretched life will end at once.'

'Well,' replied the little man, 'if you wish nothing else, you can have it, so my axe is at hand.' He quietly took his pipe from his mouth, knocked the ashes out, and put it into his pocket. Then rising slowly, he went behind the pines. But Peter sat down weeping in the grass ; his life had no longer any value for him, and he patiently awaited the deadly blow. After a short time he heard gentle steps behind him, and thought, 'Now he is coming.'

'Look up once more, Peter Munk,' cried the little man. He wiped the tears from his eyes and looked up, and beheld his mother, and Elizabeth his wife, who kindly gazed on him. Then he jumped up joyfully, saying, 'You are not dead, then, Elizabeth, nor you, mother ; and have you forgiven me ?'

'They will forgive you,' said the Little

Glass Man, 'because you feel true repentance, and all shall be forgotten. Go home now, to your father's hut, and be a charcoal-burner as before; if you are active and honest, you will do credit to your trade, and your neighbours will love and esteem you more than if you possessed ten tons of gold.' Thus saying, the Little Glass Man left them. The three praised and blessed him, and went home.

The splendid house of wealthy Peter stood no longer; it was struck by lightning, and burnt to the ground, with all its treasures. But they were not far from his father's hut, and thither they went, without caring much for their great loss. But what was their surprise when they reached the hut; it was changed into a handsome farmhouse, and all in it was simple, but good and cleanly.

'This is the Little Glass Man's doing,' cried Peter.

'How beautiful!' said Frau Elizabeth; 'and here I feel more at home than in the larger house, with many servants.'

Henceforth Peter Munk became an industrious and honest man. He was content with what he had, carried on his trade cheerfully, and thus it was that he became wealthy by his own energy, and respected and beloved in the whole forest. He no longer quarrelled with his wife, he honoured his mother, and relieved the poor who came

G

to his door.   When, after twelve months, Frau Elizabeth presented him with a beautiful little boy, Peter went to the Tannenbühl, and repeated the verse as before.   But the Little Glass Man did not show himself.

'Mr. Schatzhauser,' he cried loudly, 'only listen to me.   I wish nothing but to ask you to stand godfather to my little son.'   But he received no answer, and only a short gust of wind rushed through the pines, and cast a few cones on the grass.

'Then I will take these as a remembrance, as you will not show yourself,' cried Peter, and he put them in his pocket, and returned home.   But when he took off his jacket, and his mother turned out the pockets before putting it away, four large rolls of money fell out ; and when they opened them, they found them all good and new Baden dollars, and not one counterfeit, and these were the intended godfather's gift for little Peter, from the little man in the Tannenbühl.   Thus they lived on, quietly and cheerfully ; and many a time Peter Munk, when gray-headed, would say, ' It is indeed better to be content with little, than to have wealth and a cold heart.'   C. A. F.

THE STORY OF THE CALIPH STORK

This story is from the collection called *The Caravan*, and is told by the traveller Selim.

THE Caliph Chasid of Bagdad was sitting one fine summer afternoon comfortably on his divan; he had slept a little, for it was a sultry day, and he looked quite refreshed after his nap. He smoked a long rosewood pipe, sipped now and then a little coffee which a slave poured out for him, and stroked his beard contentedly whenever he had enjoyed it. In short, it could be seen at a glance that the Caliph felt very comfortable. At such a time it was easy to approach him, as he was very good-tempered and affable, wherefore his Grand Vizier Mansor visited him every day about this time. This afternoon he came as usual, looking, however, very grave, a rare thing for him. The Caliph took the pipe out of his mouth and said : 'Why dost thou make so grave a face, Grand Vizier ?' The Grand Vizier folded his arms across his breast, bowed to his master and answered : 'Master ! whether I assume a grave appearance I know not, but down below in the palace stands a pedlar who has such fine wares that it vexes me that I have no money to spare.'

The Caliph, who had long desired to rejoice the heart of his Grand Vizier, ordered his black slave to fetch the pedlar. In a few moments the slave returned with him. He was a stout little man, swarthy in the face, and dressed in rags. He carried a box in which he had all sorts of wares, pearls, and rings, pistols with richly inlaid stocks, goblets, and combs. The Caliph and his Vizier inspected everything, and the Caliph at last bought for himself and Vizier a pair of pistols, and for the Vizier's wife a comb. As the pedlar was about to close his box again, the Caliph caught sight of a little drawer, and asked whether it also contained some wares. The pedlar pulled out the drawer, and exhibited a snuff-box containing a black powder and a piece of paper with peculiar writing on it, which neither the Caliph nor Mansor could read. 'These things were given to me one day by a merchant who found them in the streets of Mecca,' said the pedlar. 'I know not what they are ; but you may have them for a small sum, for they are of no use to me.' The Caliph, who was very fond of having old manuscripts in his library, though unable to read them, bought both paper and box and dismissed the pedlar. Still he thought he would like to know what the writing meant, and asked the Vizier if he did not know anybody who might decipher it. ' Most gracious lord and master,' answered the latter, ' near the Great Mosque lives a man called Selim the learned ; he knows all languages. Send for him ; perhaps he can explain these mysterious signs.'

The learned Selim soon arrived. 'Selim,' said the Caliph to him, ' Selim, it is said thou art very learned. Just look at this writing whether thou canst read it ; if thou canst read it, thou gettest a new robe of honour from me ; if thou canst not, thou gettest twelve boxes on the ears and twenty-five lashes on the soles of thy feet, for having been called Selim the learned without cause.' Selim bowed and said : ' Thy will be done, O Master !' For a long time he looked at the writing ; suddenly, however, he exclaimed : ' That is Latin, O Master, or let me be hung !' ' Say what it means,' demanded the Caliph, ' if it is Latin.'

Selim began to translate : ' Man who findeth this, praise Allah for his goodness. He who takes a pinch of this powder in this box and therewith says " Mutabor," can change himself into any animal, and also understand the language of animals. If he afterwards wish to resume his human form, let him bow thrice to the East and say the same word. But beware when thou art changed that thou laughest not, or the magic word will depart from thy memory for ever, and thou remainest a beast.'

When Selim the learned had read this, the Caliph was pleased beyond measure. He made the learned man swear not to reveal the secret to any one, presented him with a splendid robe, and dismissed him. Then turning to his Grand Vizier he said : 'This I call making a bargain, Mansor! How glad I am at being able to become an animal! Come to me to-morrow morning. We will then go together into the fields, take a pinch out of the box, and then listen to what is said in the air and the water, in wood and field.'

Next morning, scarcely had the Caliph Chasid breakfasted and dressed himself, when the Grand Vizier appeared as ordered, to accompany him on his walk. The Caliph put the box with the magic powder in his girdle, and having ordered his suite to remain behind, he and the Grand Vizier set out alone on the journey. They first passed through the large gardens of the Caliph, but looked in vain for any living thing on which to try the experiment. The

Vizier at last proposed to pursue their journey to a pond, where he had often seen many animals, especially storks, whose grave manners and clappings had always excited his attention.

The Caliph approved of the Vizier's proposal, and went with him towards the pond. Having arrived there, they saw a stork soberly pacing up and down looking for frogs, and chattering something now and then to itself. At the same moment they saw far up in the sky another stork hovering in this direction.

'I wager my beard, most gracious Master,' said the Grand Vizier, 'this long-legged pair are now having a pleasant talk. How would it be if we turned into storks?'

'Wisely spoken,' replied the Caliph. 'But first, let us consider how we may become men again. It is easy enough! If we bow thrice to the East, and say Muta-bor, I shall be Caliph and thou Vizier. But for heaven's sake no laughing, or we are lost.'

While the Caliph spoke thus, he saw the other stork hovering over their heads, and slowly alighting on the ground. Quickly he snatched the box from his girdle, took a hearty pinch, gave the box to the Grand Vizier, who did the like, and both exclaimed 'Mutabor!'

Then their legs shrivelled and became

thin and red, the beautiful yellow slippers of the Caliph and those of his Vizier changed into ugly storks' feet, their arms grew into wings, their necks shot up from their shoulders and reached a yard in length, their beards vanished, and soft feathers covered their bodies.

'You have a pretty beak, Mr. Grand Vizier,' said the Caliph after a surprised silence. 'By the beard of the Prophet, I have never seen such things in my life!' 'Thanks humbly,' replied the Vizier, bowing; 'but if I might dare say so, I should avow that your Highness looks almost handsomer as a stork than a Caliph. But come, if it pleases you, let us listen to our comrades yonder and hear if we really speak storkish.'

Meanwhile the other stork had reached the ground. It cleaned its feet with its beak, settled its feathers, and walked up to the first stork. The two new storks hastened to get near them, and to their surprise heard the following conversation: 'Good morning, Madam Longlegs! You are early on the meadows.' 'Thank you, dear Clapper-beak! I have been to get a little breakfast. Would you like to have a quarter of a lizard or a little leg of a frog?' 'Much obliged; but I have no appetite this morning. Besides, I have come upon quite a different errand on the meadow. I am to dance before my

father's guests to-day, and I want to prac-
tise a little quietly.'

Thereupon the young stork began to caper
about the field in peculiar movements. The
Caliph and Mansor watched her, very much
surprised. But when she stood on one leg
in a picturesque attitude, and fluttered her
wings to increase the effect, neither of them
could resist ; laughter without stopping burst
from their beaks, from which they only
recovered a long time afterwards. The
Caliph was the first to recover self-posses-
sion : 'That was a joke,' he exclaimed,
'which cannot be bought for gold. What
a pity the stupid animals should have been
scared by our laughter, else they would also
have sung, to be sure !'

But now it occurred to the Grand Vizier
that laughing during the enchantment was
forbidden. He therefore communicated his
fears to the Caliph. 'By Mecca and Medina,
that would be a bad joke if I were to remain
a stork ! Do bethink thee of the stupid
word ; I cannot recall it.'

'Three times we must bow to the East and
say : Mu—Mu—Mu.'

They turned towards the East and kept on
bowing continually till their beaks nearly
touched the ground. But, alas ! the magic
word had escaped them, and often as the
Caliph bowed, and eagerly as his Vizier
added Mu—Mu—, yet every recollection of

it had gone, and the poor Chasid and his Vizier were storks, and remained so.

Sadly the enchanted ones wandered through the fields, not knowing what to do in their misery. They could not discard their stork-plumage, nor could they return into the town and make themselves known, for who would have believed that a stork was the Caliph? and even if one had believed it, would the inhabitants of Bagdad accept a stork for a Caliph?

Thus they wandered about for several days, living miserably on the fruits of the field, which they could not swallow very well on account of their long beaks. As for lizards and frogs, their stomachs could not relish such food; besides, they were afraid of spoiling their appetite with such tit-bits. Their only pleasure in their sad situation was that they could fly, and thus they flew often to the high roofs of Bagdad to see what was going on in the town.

During the first days they remarked great uneasiness and grief in the streets. But on the fourth day of their enchantment, while sitting on the roof of the Caliph's palace, they saw down in the street below a splendid array. The drums and fifes played; a man dressed in a gold-embroidered scarlet mantle rode a richly-caparisoned horse, surrounded by a gaudy train of servants. Half Bagdad rushed about him, and everybody shouted: 'Hail, Mizra! the ruler of Bagdad!'

Then the two storks upon the roof of the palace looked at each other, and the Caliph Chasid said: 'Dost thou guess now why I am enchanted, Grand Vizier? This Mizra is the son of my mortal enemy, the mighty Magician Kaschnur, who in an evil hour swore revenge on me. But still I do not despair. Come with me, thou faithful companion of my misery; we will betake ourselves to the grave of the Prophet; perhaps at that sacred shrine the magic may be dispelled.'

They rose from the roof of the palace and flew towards Medina.

They did not succeed very well in flying, for as yet they had had very little practice. 'O Master!' sighed the Grand Vizier after a couple of hours' flight, 'with your leave I can hold out no longer, you fly too swiftly for me! Besides, it is dark already, and we should do well to seek shelter for the night.'

Chasid listened to the request of his servant; and seeing beneath them in the valley some ruins which promised a lodging, they flew towards it. The place where they had settled for the night seemed formerly to have been a castle. Splendid pillars rose from among the ruins; several chambers which were still tolerably preserved testified to the bygone splendour of the building. Chasid and his companion strolled through the passages in search of some dry nook, when suddenly the stork Mansor stopped. 'Lord and Master,' he whispered below his breath, 'is it not foolish for a Grand Vizier, and still more so for a stork to fear ghosts? Still, I feel very uneasy, for close by some one sighed and groaned quite distinctly.' The Caliph now also stopped, and heard quite plainly a low sob, which seemed rather to come from a man than an animal. Full of anxiety, he wanted to go towards the spot whence proceeded the sound of sorrow; but the Vizier seized him by the wing with his beak and begged him not to rush upon new and unknown perils. But all was of no avail. The Caliph, who bore a brave heart beneath his stork plumage, tore himself away with the loss of some feathers, and ran towards a gloomy passage. Soon he came to a door which was ajar, and behind which he heard distinct sighs and moans. He pushed open the door with his beak, but stopped on the threshold in astonishment. In the ruined chamber, which was only dimly lighted by a little iron-barred window, he saw a great night-owl sitting on the ground. Heavy tears rolled out of its large round eyes, and with a hoarse voice it uttered its moans from its hooked beak. But when it saw the Caliph and his Vizier, who had come up in the meantime, it gave a loud cry of joy. Elegantly it wiped the tears from its eye with its brown-flecked wings, and to the great amazement of both, it cried in good human Arabic : 'Welcome, ye storks ; you are a good omen to me of my deliverance, for through storks I am to be lucky, as it was once foretold me.'

When the Caliph had recovered from his astonishment, he bowed with his long neck, set his thin legs in a graceful position, and said : 'Night-owl ! from thy words I believe that I see a fellow-sufferer. But alas ! thy hope of deliverance through us is in vain. Thou wilt recognise our helplessness in hearing our tale.' The night-owl begged him to relate it, and the Caliph commenced to relate what we already know.

When the Caliph had related his story to the owl she thanked him, and said : 'Now also listen to my tale, and learn how I am no less unlucky than you are yourself. My father is the king of the Indies ; I, his only unhappy daughter, am called Lusa. That Magician Kaschnur, who has enchanted you, has also brought misfortune upon me. One day he came to my father and asked me in marriage for his son Mizra. But my father, who is a fiery man, had him thrown downstairs. The wretch knew how to approach me again under another shape,

and one day, while I was taking some refreshments in my garden, he administered
to me, disguised as a slave, a draught, which
changed me into this hideous shape. Fainting from fear, he brought me hither and
shouted with a terrible voice into my ear :
" Here shalt thou remain, detestable, ab-
horred even by beast, to thy end, or till
one of free will, himself in this horrid form,
asks thee to be his wife. And thus I
revenge myself on thee and on thy haughty
father."

'Since then many months have passed.
Lonely and sadly I live as a recluse within
these ruins, shunned by the world, a scare-
crow even to beasts : beautiful nature is
hidden from me, for I am blind by daylight,
and only when the moon pours her wan
light over these ruins does the obscuring
veil drop from my eyes.'

When the owl had finished she again
wiped her eyes with her wings, for the story
of her woes had moved her to tears.

The Caliph, by the story of the Princess,
was plunged into deep thought. ' If I am
not mistaken,' said he, ' there is between
our misfortunes a secret connection ; but
where can I find the key to this riddle ? '
The owl answered him : ' O Master ! such
is also my belief ; for once in my infancy a
wise woman foretold that a stork should
bring me a great fortune, and I know one

way by which perhaps we may free ourselves.' The Caliph was very much surprised, and asked what way she meant.
'The enchanter who has made us both
unhappy,' said she, 'comes once every
month to these ruins. Not far from here
is a hall where he holds orgies with numer-
ous companions. Often have I spied them
there. They then relate to one another
their vile deeds. Perhaps he may pronounce
the magic word which you have forgotten.'
'O dearest Princess,' exclaimed the Caliph,
'say when comes he, and where is the
hall ?'

The owl was silent a moment, and then
said : 'You must not take it ill, but only on
one condition can I fulfil your wish.' 'Speak
out, speak out,' cried Chasid. 'Command
all, everything of me.'

'It is this, that I may also become free,
which can only be if one of you offer me his
hand.'

The stork seemed somewhat taken aback
at this proposition, and the Caliph beckoned
to his servant to go out with him a
little.

'Grand Vizier,' said the Caliph outside,
'this is a sorry bargain, but you might take
her.' 'Indeed !' answered the Grand Vizier;
'that my wife when I come home may
scratch out my eyes ? Besides, I am an
old man, while you are still young and

single, and could better give your hand to
a young and fair Princess.'

'That is just it,' sighed the Caliph, whilst
sadly drooping his wings. 'Who then has
told thee that she is young and fair? It
is buying a pig in a poke.'

They consulted one with the other for a
long time. At last when the Caliph saw
that his Vizier would rather remain a stork
than wed the owl, he resolved to fulfil the
condition himself. The owl was immensely
pleased. She confessed to them that they
could not have come at a more favourable
time, for the enchanters were very likely to
assemble that night.

She quitted the chamber with the storks
to lead them to the hall. They went a long
way through a gloomy passage; at length,
through a half-fallen wall, gleamed a bright
light. Having arrived there, the owl advised them to remain perfectly quiet. They
could, through the gap near which they
stood, overlook a great hall. It was supported all round by pillars, and splendidly
decked. Many brilliant coloured lamps replaced the light of day. In the centre of
the hall was a round table, covered with
many and choice meats. Round this table
was a couch, on which sat eight men. In
one of these men the stork recognised the
pedlar who had sold them the magic powder.
His neighbour asked him to relate his latest

deeds. Amongst others he also related the story of the Caliph and his Vizier.

'What sort of word hast thou given them?' asked another enchanter. 'A very difficult Latin one, namely, "Mutabor."'

When the storks heard this at their hole in the wall they were nearly beside themselves with joy. They ran on their long legs so quickly to the threshold of the ruins that the owl could hardly follow them. There the Caliph addressed the owl with emotion : 'Deliverer of my life and of the life of my friend, accept me in eternal gratitude for thy spouse for that which thou hast done for us.' He then turned to the East. Thrice the storks bowed their long necks to the sun, which just then was rising behind the mountains. 'Mutabor!' they exclaimed ; and straightway they were changed, and in the great joy of their new-sent life master and servant fell into each other's arms laughing and crying. But who can describe their astonishment on turning round ? A lovely lady, grandly dressed, stood before them. Smiling, she gave her hand to the Caliph. 'Do you no longer recognise your night-owl?' she said. It was she. The Caliph was so charmed with her beauty and grace that he exclaimed : 'My greatest fortune was that of having been a stork.'

The three now travelled together towards Bagdad. The Caliph found in his clothes

H

not only the box with the magic powder,
but also his purse.   He therefore bought in
the nearest village what was needful for
their journey, and so they soon came to the
gates of Bagdad.   There the arrival of the
Caliph caused much surprise.   People had
believed him dead, and they therefore were
highly pleased to have again their beloved
ruler.

All the more, however, burned their hatred
towards the impostor Mizra.   They entered
the palace, and took prisoner the old enchanter
and his son.   The Caliph sent the old man
to the same chamber in the ruins that the
Princess had lived in when an owl, and had
him hanged there.   To the son, who knew
nothing of his father's art, the Caliph gave
the choice whether he would die or take snuff.
And when he chose the latter, the Grand
Vizier handed him the box.   A good strong
pinch and the magic word of the Caliph
changed him into a stork.   The Caliph had
him shut up in an iron cage and placed in
his garden.

Long and happy lived the Caliph Chasid
with his wife the Princess.   His most pleasant
hours were always those when the Grand
Vizier visited him during the afternoon, when
they very frequently spoke of their stork
adventures, and when the Caliph was very
jovial he amused himself with imitating the
Grand Vizier when he was a stork.   He

strutted up and down the chamber with stiff legs, clapped, fluttered his arms as though they were wings, and showed how vainly the latter had turned to the East crying all the while Mu—Mu. This entertainment was at all times a great pleasure to Madam Caliph and her children ; but when the Caliph kept on clapping a little too long, and nodded, and cried Mu—Mu, then the Vizier threatened him, smiling, that he would communicate to Madam Caliph what had been discussed outside the door of the Night Owl Princess.

THE STORY OF LITTLE MUCK

This story is from the same collection, and is told
by Muley, a merry young merchant.

THERE lived at Nicea, my dear
native town, a man named Little
Muck. I can still remember
him very well, although I was
very young then, especially as I once received
from my father a sound thrashing for his
sake. Little Muck was already an old man
when I knew him, and only three or four
feet high. He presented a most extraordinary appearance, and although his body was
stunted and thin, yet he had a head which
was much larger and thicker than that of
other people. He lived quite alone in a
large house, and acted as his own cook;
people, moreover, in the town would never
have known whether he was alive or dead,
for he only went out once a month, were it
not that at mid-day a powerful steam arose

from his house ; but he was often seen during the evening walking up and down his roof, and people in the street thought that his immense head only promenaded on the roof. My playmates and myself were wicked youngsters, always ready enough to mock people and laugh at them, and whenever Little Muck came out it was a holiday for us. On the day he went out we met before his house, waiting for his appearance. When the door opened, and his immense head, together with a much larger turban, peeped out, followed by his little body, dressed in a shabby little cloak, wide trousers, and a broad girdle, to which was attached a long dagger of such an immense size that people did not know whether Muck was fastened to the dagger or the dagger to him—when he came out, the air resounded with our loud cries of joy; we threw up our caps into the air and danced like maniacs round about him. Little Muck, nevertheless, bowed to us with a grave and dignified air, and marched down the street with slow steps, dragging his feet as he walked, for he wore such large and broad slippers as I had never seen before.

We boys ran after him always shouting : 'Little Muck ! Little Muck !' We had also made a little rhyme about him which we sang in honour of him now and then, namely :

'Little Muck, Little Muck,
What an awful fright you look !
In a big house you reside,
Only once a month outside.
You are a plucky dwarf, but still
Your head is almost like a hill ;
Do but just turn round and look,
Run and catch us, Little Muck ! '

We had often played this joke, and I must confess to my shame mine was the worst. I often pulled him by his cloak, and once I planted my foot on the end of his great slippers from behind, so that he fell down. This at first caused me great delight, but I soon ceased to laugh when I saw Little Muck go towards my father's house. He really entered it, and remained in it for some time. I secreted myself behind the door and saw Little Muck come out again, accompanied by my father, who held him respectfully by the hand, and took leave of him at the door, after many bows. I felt very uneasy, and remained for a long time in my hiding-place ; but at length hunger, which I dreaded still more than the thrashing, forced me to come out, and, shame-faced and with bent head, I presented myself before my father. ' I hear you have insulted the good Muck ? ' he said in a very stern voice. ' I want to tell you the history of this Muck, and I am certain you will never mock him again ; in any case, however, before or after, you will get your punishment.' This punish-

I hear you have suited the go
said in a very stern voice

ment meant twenty-five strokes, which he counted with only too great an exactness. He took his long pipe, screwed off the amber mouth-piece, and acquitted himself more vigorously of the task than he had ever done before.

After having received the five-and-twenty strokes, my father ordered me to pay attention, and related to me the story of Little Muck.

The father of Little Muck, whose real name was Mukrah, was a distinguished but poor man here in Nicea. He, too, lived in almost as solitary a manner as his son does at present. Unfortunately, he did not like him, because his dwarfed stature made him ashamed of the boy, and consequently he had him brought up in ignorance. Little Muck, when in his sixteenth year, was still a frolicsome child; and his father, a stern man, continually reproached him with still being so childish, and also on account of his ignorance and stupidity.

The old man, however, had a bad fall one day, in consequence of which he died, leaving behind little Muck, poor and ignorant. His harsh relatives, to whom the deceased owed more than he was able to pay, turned the poor little fellow out of the house, and advised him to go abroad to seek his fortune. Little Muck said that he was already prepared for the journey; and only asked to be

allowed to take his father's clothes with him,
to which they agreed. His father had been
a tall, powerful man, and therefore his
clothes did not fit him. Muck, however,
soon devised an expedient ; he cut off all
that was superfluous with respect to length,
and then donned the garments. He seemed,
however, to have forgotten the curtailing of
them in their amplitude, hence his whimsical
attire, which he wears to this day ; the large
turban, the broad girdle, the wide trousers,
the little blue cloak, all these are heirlooms
of his father, which he has always worn ; his
father's long Damascus dagger he planted
in his girdle, and with a little staff in his
hand, he set out on his journey.

Joyfully he walked along all day, for he
had set out to seek his fortune. If he saw
a bit of broken glass on the road glittering
in the sunshine, he would put it into his
pocket, really believing it would turn into
the most beautiful diamond. If he saw in
the distance the glittering cupolas of a
mosque, or the sea smooth as glass, he
would hasten towards it joyously, thinking
he had arrived in some enchanted country.
But alas ! These phantoms disappeared as
he approached them, and only too soon did
his fatigue and the complaints of his hungry
stomach remind him that he was still in the
land of mortals.

Thus he had travelled for two days,

hungry, weary, and in despair, endeavouring
to seek his fortune; the fruits of the field
were his only food, the hard earth his couch.
On the morning of the third day he perceived from the top of a hill a large town.
The Crescent glittered upon the cupolas,
coloured banners floated upon the roofs,
seeming to beckon Little Muck to come
to them. He stood still a moment quite
surprised, looking upon the town and its
environs. 'Yes, that is the place where
Little Muck will make his fortune,' he said
to himself; and notwithstanding his weari-
ness he stepped forward, 'there or nowhere.'
He summoned up all his strength and strode
towards the city. But although it appeared
so close, he did not reach it till mid-day, for
his little legs almost entirely refused their
office, so that he was obliged to sit down
frequently under the shade of a palm-tree to
take rest. At length he reached his destina-
tion. He arranged his little cloak, improved
the position of his turban, broadened his
girdle still more, and planted his long dagger
in a still more oblique position; he then
wiped the dust from his shoes, armed himself with his little staff, and bravely entered
the city.

He had already strolled through many
streets, but nowhere a door opened
to him, nowhere people called out to
him as he had imagined: 'Little Muck,

come in, eat and drink, and rest your tiny legs.'

He was again looking up very longingly before a large and beautiful house, when a window opened, an old woman looked out of it, and exclaimed in a singing voice :

> ' Come on, come on,
> The broth is done ;
> Laid is the cloth,
> Enjoy the broth ;
> Neighbours come,
> The broth is done.'

The door of the house opened, and Muck saw many dogs and cats go into the house. He remained for some moments in a state of uncertainty, as to whether he should respond to the invitation ; at length, however, he summoned up sufficient courage and entered the house. Before him trotted a pair of young cats. He determined to follow them, because they might know the way to the kitchen better than he.

When Muck had reached the top of the stairs, he met the old woman who had looked out of the window. She looked at him sulkily, and demanded of him what he wanted. ' I have heard you inviting everybody to your feast,' answered little Muck, ' and as I am terribly hungry I have come as well.' The old woman laughed and said : ' Where do you come from, you strange creature ? The whole town knows

that I cook for nobody except my dear
cats, and now and again I invite company
from the neighbourhood for them, as you
see.' Little Muck related to the old woman
how badly he had fared after his father's
death, and entreated her to allow him to
feast this day with her cats. The woman,
who seemed pleased at the unaffected story
of the little man, allowed him to be her
guest, and gave him plenty to eat and
drink. After having regaled himself, the
woman looked at him for a long time and
then said : ' Little Muck, remain in my
service, you will have little to do and plenty
to eat.' Little Muck, who seemed to have
enjoyed the cats' broth, agreed, and thus
became Madam Ahavzi's servant. His
work was light but strange. Lady Ahavzi
owned two cats and four kittens. Little
Muck had to brush their fur and anoint
them with precious ointment every morning ;
if their mistress was absent, he had to take
care of them ; at their meals he had to
wait upon them, and at night put them
upon silk cushions and wrap them up in
velvet coverlets.

There were besides some little dogs in
the house which he also had to wait upon,
but not so much attention was bestowed
upon these as upon the cats, who were
treated like Lady Ahavzi's own children.
Altogether, Muck now lived almost as

solitarily as when he was in his late father's
house; for, with the exception of his mistress,
he only saw, during the whole day, cats
and dogs. For a short time little Muck
fared very well, he had always plenty to
eat and little to do, and the old woman
seemed to be quite satisfied with him; but
by degrees the cats became troublesome;
whenever the old lady was out they bounded
about the room like mad, setting everything
pell-mell, and breaking many valuable vases
which stood in their way. But when they
heard their mistress coming up the stairs
they crept up to their cushions, wagging
their little tails to welcome her as if nothing
had occurred. Lady Ahavzi then became
angry on seeing her rooms in such a dis-
ordered state, blaming Muck for it; and
however much he might protest his innocence, she had more confidence in her
cats, which looked so innocent, than in her
own servant.

Little Muck was very sad that he had
not found his fortune here, and resolved to
quit the service of Madam Ahavzi. But
as he had discovered during his former
travels how difficult it was to live without
money, he determined to obtain his wages,
which his mistress had always promised,
but never given him, by some means or
other. In the house of Madam Ahavzi was
a chamber which was always locked, and

the interior of which he had never seen. He had, however, often heard the woman making a noise in it, and for the life of him he would have liked to know what she kept hidden there. While thinking of his money for travelling, it occurred to him that it was probably there that Madam Ahavzi kept her treasures. The door, however, was always firmly locked, and he was unable therefore to get near them.

One morning, after Madam Ahavzi had gone out, one of the little dogs which had always been treated by her very badly, whose favour, however, he had gained in a high degree by showing it many acts of kindness, pulled him by his full trousers, and made signs to him as if to induce Muck to follow him. Muck, who had always been fond of playing with the little dog, followed it, and behold, the little dog conducted him into the bedroom of Madam Ahavzi, and to a little door which he had never seen there before. The door was ajar. The little dog went in, Muck following it, and he was agreeably surprised to find himself in the room which had been so long the aim of his wishes. He spied in every corner to see if he could find any money, but all in vain. Only old clothes and strangely-shaped vases were lying about. One of these vases especially attracted his attention. It was of crystal, and beautiful figures were cut on it. He took it up and turned it about on all sides. But, oh terror ! He had not noticed that it had a cover which was only lightly placed upon it. The cover dropped, and broke into a thousand pieces.

For a long time Little Muck stood there petrified with fear. His fate was now decided, and nothing remained for him but to run away, otherwise the old woman would kill him. He immediately determined upon going, but once more he looked round to see if he could make use of some of Lady Ahavzi's property. His eyes fell on a mighty pair of slippers. They were not very pretty, but his own could not stand another journey. They also attracted his attention on account of their immense size, for if his feet were once in them, all must plainly see that he had discarded children's boots. He quickly took off his little slippers, and put on the big ones. A pretty little staff with a lion's head carved on its top seemed also to be standing idle in the corner, so taking possession of it, he hastened out of the room. He then went quickly to his room, donned his little cloak, put on his paternal turban, planted the dagger in his girdle, and ran as fast as his legs could carry him, out of the house and the gates of the town.

Outside the town he kept on running, being afraid of the old woman, until at last he was overcome by fatigue. Never in all

his life had he gone so fast, nay, it seemed
to him as if he could go on continually, for
some invisible power seemed to urge him
on. He perceived at last that his slippers
were under the influence of some charm, for
they kept on stepping forward, and dragging
him along. He tried by all sorts of means
to stand still, but all in vain. At last, being
in the greatest danger, he called out just as
if he were guiding horses : ' Ho ! ho ! halt
ho !' The slippers immediately pulled up,
and Muck threw himself exhausted on the
ground.

He was immensely pleased with the slippers. After all, he had acquired something
by his work, which might assist him on his
way in the world, to make his fortune. In
spite of his joy he fell asleep from fatigue,
for the little body of Mr. Muck, which had
to carry such an enormous head, was not
very strong. In a dream the little dog
which had assisted him in obtaining the
slippers in Madam Ahavzi's house appeared
to him and said : ' Dear Muck, you do not
seem properly to understand the use of the
slippers : Learn, if you turn in them three
times on your heel, you can fly wherever
you like, and with the little cane you can
discover treasures : for wherever there is
gold buried it will strike the ground three
times, and where silver lies twice.'

Thus dreamt Little Muck. When he was

awake he meditated upon the strange dream, and soon resolved to make a trial. He put on the slippers, lifted one foot in the air and turned himself about on the other. Whoever has tried the feat of turning round thrice successively in a slipper too large for him will not be astonished at hearing that Little Muck did not succeed very well in his first attempt, especially if one takes into consideration that his enormous head sometimes dragged him to the right and sometimes to the left.

The poor little fellow fell several times heavily on his nose; nevertheless he did not allow himself to be discouraged from repeating the experiment, and finally he succeeded. Like a wheel he turned round on his heel, wishing himself to be transported to the nearest large town, whereupon his slippers lifted him up into the air, fled through the clouds as if they had wings, and before he could recover his senses he found himself in a large market-place, where many booths were pitched, and where a number of people were busily running to and fro. He went about amongst the people, but found it advisable to go into a more quiet street, for in the market-place people put their feet upon his slippers, which nearly made him fall down; and further, his long dagger every now and then pushed against some one or other, so that he just escaped being beaten.

Little Muck now began seriously to think what he could do to earn some money. Though he had a little staff indicating to him hidden treasures, yet where could he discover a place, on the spur of the moment, where gold or silver was buried? He might have exhibited himself in case of necessity, but he was too proud for that. At length the quick movements of his limbs occurred to him. 'Perhaps,' he thought, 'my slippers may support me,' and he resolved to offer his services as courier, thinking it possible that the King of this town might remunerate him handsomely for such services, and he inquired after the palace. Near the gate of the palace stood a sentry, who asked him what he wanted. He said that he was looking for work, and was shown to the overseer of the slaves. He told the latter his request, and petitioned him to find him a place amongst the royal messengers. The overseer looked at him from head to foot, and said : 'What! you, with your little limbs, which are scarcely a span in length, wish to become a royal messenger! Get away, I have no time for joking with a fool.'

Little Muck, however, assured him that he was quite in earnest with his offer, and that he would venture a wager to outstrip the swiftest runner. The affair seemed very ridiculous to the overseer. He ordered him to be prepared for a race in the evening, took him into the kitchen, and took care that he was supplied with plenty to eat and drink. The overseer himself went to the King, and told him about this little man and his offer. The King, who was a pleasant master, approved of the overseer for having kept Little Muck for a joke. He ordered him to make preparations on a large meadow behind the palace in order that the race might be conveniently seen by his whole royal household, and finally told him to look well after the dwarf.

The King related to the Princes and Princesses what sort of an entertainment they would have in the evening. The latter told their servants of it, and as the evening approached, all were in eager expectation; they hastened towards the meadow, where scaffolds were erected, in order to see the boasting dwarf run.

After the King, his sons and his daughters had taken their seats, Little Muck appeared upon the meadow, saluting the assemblage with an extremely courteous bow. General shouts of joy resounded on the little man appearing; such a figure had never been seen there before. The little man's body with its immense head, his little cloak and large trousers, the long dagger in the broad girdle, his little feet in his slippers: No! this was too funny a sight

for people not to laugh. Little Muck, however, did not allow himself to be abashed
by the laughter. He proudly took his
place, leaning on his little cane, and awaited
his adversary. The overseer of the slaves
had, at Muck's request, selected the quickest
runner. The latter now came forward,
placing himself by the side of the little man,
and both waited for the signal. Then the
Princess Amarza, as had been arranged,
nodded from under her veil, and like two
arrows shot at the same target, the runners
rushed forward over the meadow.

At first Muck's adversary had a decided
advantage, but the former on his slipper-
conveyance chased him, overtook him,
passed him, and reached the goal long
before the other came along gasping for
breath. The spectators were for some
moments stupefied with admiration and
astonishment, but when first the King ap-
plauded, then the whole multitude followed
his example, and all shouted :

'Long live Little Muck, the winner of the
race!'

In the meantime Little Muck had been
fetched. He prostrated himself before the
King, and said : 'All powerful King, this is
merely a trifle of my art ; and now conde-
scend to assign me a place amongst your
couriers.' The King replied : 'No, you
shall be my private runner, and always

about me. You shall have for your salary a hundred gold pieces annually, and you shall dine with my chief courtiers.'

Muck now at last thought he had found his fortune, which he had sought after for so long a time, and rejoiced inwardly. He also rejoiced at the special favour of the King, for the latter employed him for the quickest and most secret despatches, which Little Muck executed with the greatest exactitude, and with incomprehensible rapidity.

The other servants, however, were jealous of him, because they thought themselves lessened in the favour of their master, through a dwarf, who understood nothing else but running. Many conspiracies, therefore, were plotted against him in order to ruin him; but all failed, on account of the great confidence which the King placed in his chief private runner, for he had risen to this dignity in a short time.

Muck, who was not blind to these intrigues, did not think of avenging himself; he was too noble-hearted for that. No, he rather thought of some means by which he might make himself indispensable, and liked by his enemies. He then recollected his little staff, which he had forgotten in his fortunate circumstances; if he discovered treasures, he thought, then perhaps his companions might look upon him with a more favourable eye.

He had often been told that the father of the present King had buried a great part of his treasures at a time when the enemy invaded his country; it was also said that he had died since, without having been able to communicate his secret to his son. Henceforward Muck always took his little cane with him, hoping that some day he might pass the place where the money of the old King lay buried. One evening chance led him to a lonely spot in the King's garden, a place which he little frequented, when suddenly he felt his little cane jerking in his hand, and striking the ground three times. He was already aware what this meant. He therefore drew his dagger, notched the trees surrounding the place, and returned to the castle: he now procured a spade, and waited until nightfall for his enterprise.

His searching for the treasures gave Little Muck more trouble than he had expected. His arms were very weak, his spade too large and heavy, and he worked for more than two hours before he had dug two feet in depth. At length he struck against something hard, which gave a metallic sound. He now dug away more vigorously, and soon succeeded in bringing to light a large iron lid; he himself got into the hole in order to discover what the lid might cover, and he really found a large urn filled with gold pieces. His feeble powers, however, were insufficient to lift the urn, and he therefore put into his trousers and girdle as much as he could carry ; he stuffed his little cloak with as much as he could, and put it on his back, having concealed the rest very carefully. But, as a matter of fact, if he had not had his slippers on, he would not have been able to proceed, so heavily the gold weighed on him. Unobserved, he reached his room, and there concealed his gold underneath the cushions of his couch.

When Little Muck found himself the owner of so much gold he thought matters would now undergo a change, and that he would gain amongst his enemies at court many patrons and warm friends. Judging from this, it was but too obvious that Little Muck could not have received a very careful education, otherwise he would not have imagined that it was possible to gain real friends with gold. Alas ! he had much better have greased his slippers then, and made his escape with his little cloak filled with gold as quickly as he could.

The gold which Little Muck now freely distributed excited the jealousy of the other courtiers. The chief cook Ahuli said : ' He is a coiner.' Achmet, the overseer of the slaves, said : ' He has obtained it from the King by talking.' Archaz, the treasurer, however, his bitterest enemy, who himself from time to time dipped into the King's cash-box, said openly: 'He has stolen it.' Now in order to make quite sure of their affair, they plotted together, and the chief cup-bearer Korchuz presented himself one day very sad and downcast before the King. He dissimulated in such a way that the King asked him what was the matter with him. 'Alas!' he answered, 'I am sad for having lost the grace of my master.' 'What are you raving about, friend Korchuz?' said the King. 'How long has the sunshine of my favour ceased to fall on you?' The chief cup-bearer answered him that he had lavished so much gold on his private chief runner, and forgotten him, his poor and faithful servant, altogether.

The King was much astonished at this news, and caused little Muck's distributions of gold to be related to him, and the conspirators easily made him suspect that Muck by some means or other had stolen the money from the treasury. The treasurer was very pleased at this turn of affairs, and besides, was reluctant to give an account of the state of his books. The King therefore ordered them to watch all the movements of Little Muck, in order to surprise him if possible in the act of stealing. When, therefore, during the night following this fatal day, Little Muck took the spade in order to go into the King's garden to get a fresh supply from his secret treasure, because he had exhausted his store through his liberality, he was followed by the sentries, headed by the chief cook Ahuli and the treasurer Archaz; and just as he was about to put the gold into his little cloak they attacked him, bound him, and brought him immediately before the King. The latter, whose disturbed slumbers had not put him in a very good humour, received his poor chief private runner very ungraciously, and examined him immediately. The pot had been dug completely out of the ground, and with the spade, as well as the little cloak filled with gold, had been placed before the King. The treasurer alleged that he had surprised Muck with his sentinels at the moment when he had buried this pot of gold in the ground.

The King questioned the accused as to whether it was true, and where he had got the gold which he had buried. Little Muck assured him of his innocence, and said that he had discovered this pot in the garden, and that he was not going to bury it, but to dig it out.

All present laughed at this excuse; the King, however, greatly exasperated at the barefaced impudence of the little man, exclaimed: 'You wretch! You dare to impose on your King in such a gross fashion, after having robbed him? Treasurer Archaz,

I call upon you to say whether you recognise this sum of gold as the same which is missing from my treasury?' The treasurer said he was quite sure that so much and still more had been missing for some time from the royal treasury, and that he was prepared to affirm it with an oath that this was the stolen money.

Thereupon the King ordered Little Muck to be put in heavy chains and taken to the tower; the gold he gave to the treasurer, in order to restore it to the treasury. Delighted at the fortunate result of the affair, he left, and counted the glittering gold pieces at home; but the bad man never announced that there had been at the bottom of the pot a piece of paper on which was written: 'The enemy has inundated my country, therefore I bury here part of my treasures; whoever the finder may be is cursed by the King if he does not immediately deliver it up to my son. King Sadi.'

Little Muck made sad reflections in his prison; he knew that death was the punishment for stealing the King's property, yet he did not intend to reveal the secret of the little staff to the King, fearing he should be deprived of it as well as of his slippers. His slippers could not assist him at all, for he was chained close to a wall, and could not, in spite of his endeavours, turn round on his heel. When, however, on the next day he was informed that he had to die, he thought it best after all to live without the magic wand rather than die with it, so he requested the King for a private interview, and revealed to him the secret. The King at first had not much faith in his confession; but Little Muck promised a trial if the King assured him that he should not be killed. The King gave him his word for it, and, unknown to Muck, had some gold buried in the ground, and told him to find it with his little staff. In a few moments he had discovered it, for the little staff struck three times distinctly upon the ground. The King now recognised that his treasurer had deceived him, and sent him, as is customary in the East, a silk cord to hang himself with. But to Little Muck he said: 'Although I have promised to spare your life, yet it seems to me you possess more than the secret of this little staff; therefore you shall pass the rest of your days in captivity, unless you reveal the means by which you run so swiftly.'

Little Muck, for whom one night in the tower had been sufficient to make him hate captivity, confessed that all his art lay in his slippers; but he did not tell the King the secret of turning three times on the heel. The King himself slipped into the slippers in order to make a trial, and rushed about

like a madman in his garden ; he often
wanted to stop, but he did not know how it
was possible, and Little Muck, who could
not help avenging himself a little, allowed
him to run until he fell down fainting.

When the King had gained consciousness
again, he was terribly angry with Little Muck
for having let him run about breathless. ' I
have pledged my word to set you at liberty,
and to spare your life. Quit my kingdom
within twelve hours, else I will have you
hung.' The slippers and the little staff,
however, were put into his treasury.

As poor as before, Little Muck left the
country, cursing his folly which had deceived
him in imagining that he might play a
prominent part at Court. Fortunately, the
country from which he was banished was
not extensive, and after eight hours he
reached the frontier, although he had some
difficulty in walking, for he was accustomed
to his dear slippers.

After he had crossed the frontier he struck
out of the main path to find the most solitary
spot of the forest, intending to live there
only for himself, for he hated all mankind.
In a dense forest he chanced upon a little
place, which seemed quite suitable to him
according to the plan which he had formed.
A clear stream, surrounded by gigantic and
shady fig-trees and a soft piece of turf, invited
him to throw himself down, and it was here

that he intended to take no more nourish-
ment, but to await death. Over these reflections of death he fell asleep ; but on awaking,
and when hunger tormented him, he came
to the conclusion that after all to die of
hunger was a terrible thing, and looked
around to see if he could find anything
to eat.

There were some delicious ripe figs on the
tree under which he had slept, so he climbed
up the tree to gather some, enjoyed them
heartily, and then came down to quench his
thirst in the brook. But how great was his
terror when his reflection in the water
showed him his head ornamented with two
immense ears and a thick long nose. In
dismay he seized his ears with his hands ;
indeed they were more than half a yard long.

' I deserve donkey's ears ! ' he exclaimed,
' for I have, like an ass, trampled upon my
fortune.' He wandered amongst the trees,
and on feeling hungry again, he ate once
more of the figs, for there was nothing else
eatable on the trees. Whilst he was eating
the second lot of figs it occurred to him that
there might be room enough for his ears
under his great turban, so as not to appear
too ridiculous ; but he felt that his ears had
disappeared ! He immediately returned to
the brook, in order to make sure of it. And
indeed it was true ; his ears had assumed
their former appearance, and also his long

and unshapely nose had changed. He now
perceived how all this had happened ; it was
owing to the figs from the first tree that he
had got the long nose and ears ; the second
had healed him. Gladly he recognised that
his good fortune had once again given him
the means of being happy. He therefore
gathered from each tree as much as he could
carry, and returned to the country which he
had recently quitted. In the first little town
he entered he disguised himself, and without
stopping went towards the city where the
King resided, and soon arrived there.

It happened to be the season of the year
when ripe fruits were scarce ; Little Muck
therefore sat down near the gate of the
palace, for he remembered that in former
times the chief cook bought such rarities for
the royal table. Muck had only just sat
down when he saw the chief cook coming
across the court. He inspected the wares
of the sellers who had collected near the
gate of the palace ; at last his attention was
directed towards Muck's little basket. ' Ah !
a rare bit,' he said, ' which His Majesty will
certainly enjoy. How much do you want
for the whole basketful ? ' Little Muck asked
a moderate price, and they were soon agreed
over the bargain. The chief cook gave the
basket to a slave and continued his way.
Little Muck, however, ran away in the meantime, for he feared that if the horrible

developments were to appear on the heads of those at Court, he being the seller might be sought out and punished.

The King was in high spirits during dinner, and complimented the chief cook over and over again on account of his excellent cooking, and care in always selecting the best for him. The chief cook, however, who was well aware what delicacy was yet to come, smiled significantly, and merely said, 'The day is not over yet,' or 'All's well that ends well,' so that the Princesses became very curious what else was to come. When, therefore, he had the splendid inviting figs served up, there was a universal cry of 'Ah!' from all present. 'How beautiful, how inviting!' exclaimed the King. 'Chief cook, you are a capital fellow, and worthy of our entire favour.' In speaking thus the King himself distributed these delicacies, with which he was always very frugal, to every one at table. Each Prince and each Princess received two, the ladies in waiting, the viziers, and the officers one each, the rest he placed before himself, and commenced to eat them with a good appetite.

'But dear me, how peculiar you look, father!' exclaimed Princess Amarza all at once. All looked at the King in surprise: immense ears hung down on his head, a long nose extended down his chin. All the guests looked at each other with astonishment and terror; all were more or less adorned with this peculiar head-dress.

The consternation of the Court may be easily imagined. They immediately sent for all the physicians in the town, who came in troops, prescribed pills and mixtures, but the ears and noses remained. An operation was performed on one of the Princes, but the ears budded out again.

Muck had heard of the whole affair in his hiding-place, and thought now was the time for him to act. He had already procured for himself a dress with the money which he had obtained for the figs, and now appeared as a wise man. A long beard of goat's hair disguised him completely. He entered the palace of the King with a little bag filled with figs, and offered his services as a foreign physician. At first they were somewhat sceptical, but after Little Muck had given a fig to one of the Princes to eat, and when the latter's ears and nose again assumed their original shape, then all desired to be cured by the foreign physician. The King, however, took him silently by the hand and led him into his apartment; he there unlocked a door which led into the treasury, beckoning Muck to follow him. 'Here are my treasures,' said the King; 'make your selection, and whatever it be, you shall have, if you rid me of this frightful evil.' This was sweet music to the ears of Little

Muck ; immediately on entering he had seen his slippers lying on the floor, together with his little staff. He now went about the room as if he were desirous of admiring the King's treasures. Scarcely, however, had he come to his slippers when he quietly slipped into them, seized his little staff, tore off his false beard, and displayed to the amazed King the well-known features of the exiled Muck. 'Perfidious King,' he said, ' who repay with ingratitude faithful services, take as a well-deserved punishment the deformity which has overtaken you. You shall wear the long ears in order that they may remind you daily of Little Muck.'

After having said this he quickly turned round on his heel, wishing himself far away, and before the King was able to call for assistance Little Muck was out of sight. Ever since Little Muck lives here in great wealth, but secluded, for he hates men. Experience has taught him wisdom, and notwithstanding his strange exterior, he rather deserves your admiration than your mockery.

That is the story which my father told me. I repented of my unworthy conduct towards the good little man, and my father remitted the other half of the punishment which was yet in store for me. I related to my comrades the marvellous adventures of the little man, and we became so fond of him that none of us ever mocked him again. On the contrary, we respected him as long as he lived, and always bowed to him with as much respect as we should have done before a Cadi or a Mufti.

K

NOSE, THE DWARF

This story is from the collection called *The Sheik of Alexandria and his Slaves,* and is told by a slave to the Sheik.

SIR, those people are much mistaken who fancy that there were no fairies and enchanters, except in the time of Haroun Al Raschid, Lord of Bagdad, or even pronounce those accounts untrue of the deeds of genii and their princes, which one hears the story-tellers relate in the market-places of the town. There are fairies nowadays, and it is but a short time since I myself was witness of an occurrence in which genii were evidently playing a part, as you will see from my narrative. In a considerable town of my dear fatherland, Germany, there lived many years ago a cobbler, with his wife, in a humble but honest way. In the daytime he used to sit at the corner of a street mending shoes and slippers; he did not refuse making new ones if anybody would trust him, but he was obliged to buy the leather first, as his poverty did not enable him to keep a stock. His wife sold vegetables and fruit, which she cultivated in a small garden outside the town-gates, and many people were glad to buy of her, because she was dressed cleanly and neatly, and knew how to arrange and lay out her things to the best advantage.

Now this worthy couple had a beautiful boy, of a sweet countenance, well made, and rather tall for his age, which was eight years. He was in the habit of sitting in the market with his mother, and often carried home part of the fruit and vegetables for the women and cooks who had made large purchases; he seldom, however, returned from one of these journeys without bringing either a beautiful flower, a piece of money, or a cake, which the mistresses of such cooks gave him as a present, because they were always pleased to see the handsome boy come to the house.

One day the cobbler's wife was sitting as usual in the market-place, having before her some baskets with cabbages and other vegetables, various herbs and seeds, besides some early pears, apples, and apricots, in a small basket. Little Jacob (this was the boy's name) sat by her, crying out in a loud voice: 'This way, gentlemen, see what beautiful cabbages, what fragrant herbs; early pears, ladies, early apples and apricots; who will buy? My mother sells cheap.'

While the boy was thus calling out, an old woman came across the market; her dress was tattered and in rags, she had a small, sharp face, quite furrowed with age, red eyes, and a pointed, crooked nose, which reached down to her chin; in her walk she supported herself on a long stick, and yet it was difficult to say exactly how she walked, for she hobbled and shuffled along, and waddled as if she were on casters, and it was as if she must fall down every instant and break her pointed nose on the pavement.

The cobbler's wife looked attentively at this old woman. For sixteen years she had been sitting daily in the market, yet she had never observed this strange figure, and therefore involuntarily shuddered when she saw the old hag hobbling towards her and stopping before her baskets.

'Are you the greengrocer Hannah?' she asked in a disagreeable, croaking voice, shaking her head to and fro.

'Yes, I am,' replied the cobbler's wife; 'what is your pleasure?'

'We'll see, we'll see, we'll look at your herbs — look at your herbs, to see whether you have what I want,' answered the old woman; and stooping down she thrust her dark brown, unsightly hands into the herb-basket, and took up some that were beautifully spread out, with her long spider-like fingers, bringing them one by one up to her long nose, and smelling them all over. The poor woman felt her heart quake when she saw the old hag handle her herbs in this manner, but she dared not say anything to her, the purchasers having a right to examine the things as they pleased; besides which, she felt a singular awe in the presence of this old woman. After having searched the whole basket, she muttered, 'Wretched stuff, wretched herbs, nothing that I want —were much better fifty years ago — wretched stuff! wretched stuff!'

Little Jacob was vexed at these words. 'Hark ye,' he cried boldly, 'you are an impudent old woman; first you thrust your nasty brown fingers into these beautiful herbs and squeeze them together, then you hold them up to your long nose, so that no one seeing this will buy them after you, and you abuse our goods, calling them wretched stuff, though the duke's cook himself buys all his herbs of us.'

The old woman leered at the bold boy, laughed disagreeably, and said in a hoarse voice, 'Little son, little son, you like my nose then, my beautiful long nose? You shall have one too in the middle of your face that shall reach down to your chin.'

While she spoke thus she shuffled up to another basket containing cabbages. She took the most beautiful white heads up in her hand, squeezed them together till they squeaked, and then throwing them into the basket again without regard to order, said as before, 'Wretched things! wretched cabbages!'

'Don't wriggle your head about in that ugly fashion,' cried the little boy, rather frightened; 'why your neck is as thin as a cabbage-stalk and might easily break, then your head would fall into the basket, and who would buy of us?'

'You don't like such thin necks then, eh?' muttered the old woman, with a laugh. 'You shall have none at all; your head shall be fixed between your shoulders, that it may not fall down from the little body.'

'Don't talk such nonsense to the little boy,' at length said the cobbler's wife, indignant at the long-looking, examining, and smelling of the things; 'if you wish to buy anything be quick, for you scare away all my other customers.'

'Well, be it as you say,' cried the old woman, with a furious look; 'I will buy these six heads of cabbages; but you see I must support myself on my stick, and cannot

carry anything, therefore allow your little
son to carry them home for me, and I will
reward him.'

The little boy would not go with her, and
began to cry, for he was terrified at the ugly
old woman, but his mother commanded him
to go, as she thought it a sin to load the
feeble old soul with the burden. Still sob-
bing, he did as he was ordered, and followed
the old woman across the market-place.

She proceeded slowly, and was almost
three-quarters of an hour before she arrived
at a very remote part of the town, where
she at length stopped in front of a small
dilapidated house. She pulled out of her
pocket an old rusty hook, and thrust it
dexterously into a small hole in the door,
which immediately opened with a crash.
But what was the astonishment of little
Jacob as he entered ! The interior of the
house was magnificently adorned, the ceil-
ing and walls were of marble, the furniture
of the most beautiful ebony, inlaid with gold
and polished stones, the floor was of glass,
and so smooth that little Jacob several
times slipped and fell down. The old
woman took a small silver whistle from her
pocket, and blew a note on it which sounded
shrilly through the house. Immediately
some guinea-pigs came down the stairs, and
little Jacob was much amazed at their walking upright on their hind legs, wearing on

their paws nut-shells instead of shoes, men's clothes on their bodies, and even hats in the newest fashion on their heads.

'Where are my slippers, ye rascally crew?' cried the old woman, striking at them with her stick, so that they jumped squeaking into the air; 'how long am I to stand here waiting?'

They quickly scampered up the stairs and returned with a pair of cocoa-nut shells lined with leather, which they placed dexterously upon the old woman's feet.

Now all her limping and shuffling was at an end. She threw away her stick, and glided with great rapidity over the glass floor, drawing little Jacob after her. At length she stopped in a room which was adorned with a great variety of utensils, and which closely resembled a kitchen, although the tables were of mahogany, and the sofas covered with rich cloth, more fit for a drawing-room.

'Sit down,' said the old woman kindly, pressing him into a corner of a sofa, and placing a table before him in such a manner that he could not get out again; 'sit down, you have had a heavy load to carry; human heads are not so light—not so light.'

'But, woman,' replied the little boy, 'you talk very strangely; I am, indeed, tired, but they were cabbage heads I was carrying, and you bought them of my mother.'

'Why, you know but little about that,' said the old woman laughing, as she took the lid from the basket and brought out a human head, which she held by the hair. The little boy was frightened out of his senses at this ; he could not comprehend how it came about ; and thinking of his mother, he said to himself, ' If any one were to hear of these human heads, my mother would certainly be prosecuted.'

' I must give you some reward now, as you are so good,' muttered the old woman ; ' have patience for a minute, and I will prepare for you a soup which you will remember all your life.' Having said this, she whistled again, and immediately there came first some guinea-pigs dressed like human beings ; they had tied round them kitchen-aprons, fastened by a belt, in which were stuck ladles and carving-knives ; after them came skipping in a number of squirrels that wore large, wide Turkish trousers, walked upright, and had small caps of green velvet on their heads. These seemed to be the scullions, for they climbed very nimbly up the walls and brought down pans and dishes, eggs and butter, herbs and flour, and carried it to the hearth. The old woman slided continually to and fro upon her cocoa-nut slippers, and little Jacob observed that she was bent on cooking something good for him. Now the fire crackled and blazed up higher, there was a smoking and bubbling in the saucepan, and a pleasant odour spread over the room, but the old woman kept running up and down, the squirrels and guinea-pigs after her, and as often as she passed the hearth she poked her long nose into the pot. At length it began to boil and hiss, the steam rose from the pot, and the scum flowed down into the fire. She then took off the saucepan, and pouring some into a silver basin, gave it to Jacob.

'Now, my dear little son, now,' said she, 'eat this soup, and you will have in your own person all that you admired so much in me. You shall moreover become a clever cook, that you may be something at least, but as for the herb, that you shall never find, because your mother did not have it in her basket.'

The little boy did not exactly understand what she was saying, but was the more attentive in eating his soup, which he relished uncommonly. His mother had cooked various savoury soups, but never any like this. The flavour of the fine herbs and spice ascended from it, and it was at the same time very sweet, and very sharp and strong. While he was sipping the last drops of the delicious soup the guinea-pigs lighted some Arabian incense, which floated through the room in blue clouds, which became thicker and thicker, and then descended. The smell of the incense had a stupefying effect upon the boy; in vain he repeatedly said to himself that he must return to his mother, for as often as he endeavoured to rouse himself, as often did he relapse into slumber, and, at length, actually fell into a profound sleep upon the old woman's sofa.

Strange dreams came over him while he thus slept. It seemed as if the old woman was taking off his clothes, and putting on him the skin of a squirrel. Now he could make bounds and climb like a squirrel; he associated with the other squirrels and guinea-pigs, who were all very polite, decent people, and he did duty in waiting upon the old woman in his turn like the rest. At first he had to perform the service of a shoe-black, that is, he had to oil and polish the cocoa-nut shells which his mistress wore instead of slippers. Having often blacked and polished shoes at home, he performed his duty well and quickly. After the lapse of about one year he dreamt again (according to the sequel of his dream) that he was employed for more delicate work, that is, in company with some other squirrels, he was set to catch the motes in a sunbeam, and, when they had caught enough, to sift them through the finest hair-sieve, as the old woman considered them the nicest food, and not being able to masticate well for want of teeth, had her bread prepared of such motes.

At the end of another year he was raised to the rank of one of the servants who had to collect the water the old woman drank. But you must not suppose that she had a cistern dug for that purpose, or a tub placed in the yard to catch the rain-water; she had a much finer plan. The squirrels, and Jacob with them, had to collect in their hazel-nut shells the dew from roses, and this was the beverage of the old woman. The labour of these water-carriers was not a very light one, as she used to drink a great deal. After another year he was employed in in-door service, his duty being to clean the floors, and as they were of glass and showed the least speck, it was not a very easy task. He and his fellow-servants were obliged to brush the floors, and with pieces of old cloth tied to their feet dexterously skated about the rooms. In the fourth year he received an appointment in the kitchen, which was so honourable an office that one could succeed to it only after a long probation. Jacob here served from scullion upwards to the post of first pastrycook, and acquired such an extraordinary skill and experience in everything relating to the culinary art that often he could not help wondering at himself; the most difficult things, pies composed of two hundred different ingredients, soups prepared with all the herbs of the globe,— all these, and many other things, he learned to make quickly and efficiently.

Seven years had thus passed away in the service of the old woman when one day, pulling off her shoes of cocoa-nut, and taking her basket and crutch in hand in order to go out, she told him to pluck a chicken, stuff it with herbs, and roast it nice and brown, during her absence. He did this according to the rules of his art; twisted the chicken's neck, scalded it in hot water, pulled out the feathers cleverly, scraped its skin smooth and fine, and then drew it. Next he began gathering the herbs with which he was to stuff the chicken. Now when he came to the chamber where these herbs were kept he perceived a small cupboard in the wall that he had never before noticed, and finding the door of it half open, he had the curiosity to go near, in order to see what it contained, when behold! there stood a great many little baskets in it, from which proceeded a strong pleasant smell. He opened one of these little baskets, and found in it a herb of a most singular form and colour; its stalks and leaves were of a bluish green, and it had a flower of burning red fringed with yellow at the top. He looked thoughtfully at this flower, and smelled it, when it emitted the same powerful odour as the soup which the old woman

had cooked for him when he first came there.
But the smell was so strong that he began
to sneeze, was obliged to keep sneezing, and
at last awoke, sneezing still.

He now found himself upon the old
woman's sofa, and looked around him with
astonishment. 'Heavens!' he said to himself, 'how vividly one may dream; I would
almost have sworn that I was a wanton
squirrel,—a companion of guinea-pigs and
other animals, but at the same time had
become a great cook. How my mother will
laugh when I tell her all this! But will she
not also scold me for falling asleep in a
strange house instead of helping her in the
market?' While engaged in these thoughts
he started up to run away; but his limbs
were still quite stiff with sleep, and particularly
his neck, for he was unable to move his
head well to and fro. He could not help
smiling at himself and his drowsiness, for
every moment, before he was aware, he ran
his nose against a cupboard or the wall, or
turning suddenly round, struck it against a
door-post. The squirrels and guinea-pigs
crowded whining around him, as if anxious
to accompany him, and he actually invited
them to do so when he was on the threshold,
for they were nice little creatures, but they
glided quickly back into the house on their
nutshells, and he only heard them howling
at a distance.

As it was a very remote part of the town to which the old woman had brought him, he could hardly find his way through the narrow streets, and as, moreover, there was a great crowd of people wherever he went, he could only account for this by supposing there must be a dwarf somewhere in the neighbourhood for show, for he heard everywhere cries of, 'Only look at the ugly dwarf! Where does the dwarf come from? O! what a long nose he has, and how his head sits between his shoulders, and look at his brown ugly hands!' At any other time he would probably have followed the cry, for he was very fond of seeing giants and dwarfs, and any sort of curious, foreign costume, but now he was obliged to hurry and get to his mother.

He felt quite weary when he arrived at the market. He found his mother still sitting there, and she had a tolerable quantity of fruit in the basket; he could not therefore have been sleeping long, but still it appeared to him, even at a distance, as if she were very melancholy, for she did not call to those coming past to buy, but supported her head on one hand, and on coming closer he thought she looked paler than usual. He hesitated as to what he should do; and at length mustering up courage, crept gently behind her, and putting his hand familiarly upon her arm, asked, 'Dear mother, what's the matter with you? are you angry with me?'

The woman turned round, but started back with a shriek of terror, saying, 'What do you want with me, you ugly dwarf? Begone, begone! I do not like such jokes.'

'But mother, what is the matter with you?' asked Jacob, quite terrified; 'surely you must be unwell; why will you turn your son away from you?'

'I have told you already to be gone,' replied Hannah angrily; 'you will not get any money from me by your juggleries, you ill-favoured monster.'

'Surely God has deprived her of the light of her intellect,' said the dwarf, deeply grieved within himself; 'what shall I do to get her home? Dear mother, pray do listen to reason; only look well at me, I am indeed your son—your own Jacob.'

'Why this is carrying the joke too far,' she said to her neighbour; 'only look at that ugly dwarf; there he stands, and will no doubt drive away all my customers; nay, he even dares to ridicule my misfortune, telling me that he is my son, my own Jacob, the impudent fellow.'

At this her neighbours rose, and began abusing him (every one knows that market women understand this), and reproaching him with making light of poor Hannah's misfortune, who seven years ago had had her beautiful boy kidnapped, and with one accord they threatened to fall upon him and tear him to pieces, unless he took himself off immediately.

Poor Jacob did not know what to make of all this. Indeed it seemed to him that he had that very morning, as usual, gone to market with his mother, had helped her to lay out her fruit, and had afterwards gone with the old woman to her house, eaten some soup, slept a little while, and had now come back; and yet his mother and her neighbours talked of seven years, calling him at the same time an ugly dwarf. What then was the change that had come over him? Seeing, at length, that his mother would no longer listen to anything he said, he felt the tears come in his eyes, and went sorrowfully down the street towards the stall where his father sat in the daytime mending shoes.

'I am curious to see,' he thought to himself, 'whether he, too, will disown me? I will place myself in the doorway and talk to him.' And having come there he did so and looked in.

The cobbler was so busily engaged at work that he did not see him; but happening to cast a look towards the door, he dropped shoe, twine, and awl on the ground, and cried with astonishment, 'For Heaven's sake, what is that?'

L

'Good evening, master,' said the little dwarf, stepping inside the booth. 'How fare you?'

'Badly, badly, my little gentleman,' replied Jacob's father, to his utter amazement; for he, too, did not seem to recognise him. 'I have to do all the work myself, for I am alone and now getting old, and yet I cannot afford to keep a journeyman.'

'But have you no son to assist you in your work?' inquired the dwarf further.

'Indeed I had one, whose name was Jacob, and he now must be a handsome, quick lad, twenty years old, who might effectually assist me. Ah! what a pleasant life I should lead. Even when he was twelve years old he showed himself quite handy and clever, and understood a great deal of the business. He was a fine engaging little fellow; he would soon have brought me plenty of custom, so that I should no longer have been mending shoes and boots but making new ones. But so goes the world.'

'Where is your son, then?' asked Jacob in a tremulous voice.

'That God only knows,' replied his father. 'Seven years ago, yes! it is just that now, he was stolen from us in the market-place.'

'Seven years ago, you say?' cried Jacob with astonishment.

'Yes, little gentleman, seven years ago;

the circumstance is as fresh in my memory
as if it had happened to-day, how my poor
wife came home weeping and crying, saying
that the child had not come back all day,
and that she had inquired and searched
everywhere without finding him. But I
always said it would come to that ; for Jacob
was a pretty child, no one could help saying
so, therefore my poor wife was proud of him
and fond of hearing people praise him, and
often sent him with vegetables and such like
to the houses of the gentlefolks. All this
was very well ; he always received some
present. But said I, mark me, the town is
large, and there are many bad people in it,
so take care of Jacob. But it happened as
I said. Once there comes an ugly old
woman to the market, bargains for some
fruits and vegetables, and at length buys so
much that she cannot carry it home herself.
My wife, kind soul, sends the lad with her, and
—has never seen him again since that hour.'

'And that is now seven years ago ?'

'Seven years this spring. We had him
cried in the town, we went from house to
house inquiring ; many had known and liked
the pretty lad, and searched with us, but all
in vain. Neither did any one know the
woman who bought the vegetables ; a very
aged woman, however, ninety years old,
said, ' it might possibly have been the
wicked fairy, Kräuterweis, who once in

fifty years comes to the town to buy various
things ? '

Thus spoke Jacob's father hastily, ham-
mering at his shoes meanwhile, and drawing
out at great length the twine with both hands.
Now by degrees light broke on the little
dwarf, and he saw what had happened to
him, viz., that he had not been dreaming,
but had served as a squirrel seven years with
the evil fairy. Rage and sorrow filled his
heart almost to bursting.

The old witch had robbed him of seven
years of his youth, and what had he in ex-
change ? What was it that he could polish
slippers of cocoa-nut shell ? that he could
clean rooms with glass floors ? that he had
learned all the mysteries of cooking from
the guinea-pigs ? Thus he stood for some
time meditating on his fate, when at length
his father asked him—

' Do you want to purchase anything,
young gentleman ? Perhaps a pair of new
slippers or, peradventure, a case for your
nose ? ' he added, smiling.

' What do you mean about my nose ? '
asked Jacob ; ' why should I want a case
for it ? '

' Why,' replied the cobbler, ' every one
according to his taste ; but I must tell you
that if I had such a terrible nose I should
have a case made for it of rose-coloured
morocco. Look here, I have a beautiful

piece that is just the thing; indeed we should at least want a yard for it. It would then be well guarded, my little gentleman; whereas now I am sure you will knock it against every door-post and carriage you would wish to avoid.'

The dwarf was struck dumb with terror; he felt his nose; it was full two hands long, and thick in proportion. So then the old hag had likewise changed his person; and hence it was his mother did not know him, and people called him an ill-favoured dwarf.

'Master,' said he, half crying to the cobbler, 'have you no looking-glass at hand in which I might behold myself?'

'Young gentleman,' replied his father gravely, 'you have not exactly been favoured as to appearance so as to make you vain, and you have no cause to look often in the glass. You had better leave it off altogether. It is with you a particularly ridiculous habit.'

'Oh! pray let me look in the glass,' cried the dwarf. 'I assure you it is not from vanity.'

'Leave me in peace, I have none in my possession; my wife has a little looking-glass, but I do not know where she has hid it. If you really must look into one,—why then, over the way lives Urban, the barber, who has a glass twice as big as your head; look in there, and now, good morning.'

With these words his father pushed him

gently out of the stall, locked the door after him, and sat down again to his work.   The little dwarf, much cast down, went over the way to the barber, whom he well remembered in former times.

'Good morning, Urban,' said he to him, 'I come to beg a favour of you ; be so kind as to let me look a moment in your looking-glass.'

'With pleasure,' cried the barber laughing ; 'there it is,' and his customers who were about to be shaved laughed heartily with him.   'You are rather a pretty fellow, slim and genteel ; you have a neck like a swan, hands like a queen, and a turn-up nose, such as one seldom sees excelled.   A little vain you are of it, no doubt ; but no matter, look at yourself ; people shall not say that envy prevented me from allowing you to see yourself in my glass.'

Thus spoke the barber, and a yell of laughter resounded through the room.   In the meantime the dwarf had stepped to the glass and looked at himself.   The tears came in his eyes while saying to himself : 'Yes, dear mother, thus you could not indeed recognise your Jacob ; he did not look like this in the days of your happiness, when you delighted to show him off before the people ?' His eyes had become little, like those of a pig ; his nose was immense, hanging over his mouth down to his chin ; his neck

seemed to have been taken away altogether,
for his head sat low between his shoulders,
and it was only with the greatest pain that
he could move it to the right or left ; his
body was still the same size as it had been
seven years ago, when he was twelve years
old, so that he had grown in width what
others do in height between the ages of
twelve and twenty. His back and chest
stood out like two short, well-filled bags ;
and this thick-set body was supported by
small thin legs, which seemed hardly sufficient to support their burden ; but so much
the larger were his arms, which hung down
from his body, being of the size of those of
a full-grown man ; his hands were coarse,
and of a brownish hue, his fingers long, like
spiders' legs, and when he stretched them
to their full extent he could touch the
ground without stooping. Such was little
Jacob's appearance, now that he had been
turned into an ugly dwarf. He remembered
the morning on which the old woman had
stopped before his mother's baskets. All
that he then had found fault with in her—
viz., her long nose and ugly fingers—all
these she had given him, only omitting her
long, palsied neck.

'Well, my prince, have you looked
enough at yourself now?' said the barber,
stepping up to him, and surveying him with
a laugh. 'Truly, if we wished to dream of

such a figure, we could hardly see one so comical. Nevertheless I will make you a proposition, my little man. My shaving-room is tolerably well frequented, but yet not so much as I could wish. That arises from my neighbour, the barber Schaum, having discovered a giant, who attracts much custom to his house. Now, to become a giant is no great thing, after all, but to be such a little man as you is indeed a different thing. Enter my service, little man; you shall have board and lodging, clothes, and everything; for this you shall stand in my doorway in the morning, and invite people to come in; you shall beat the lather, hand the towel to the customers, and you may be sure that we shall both make it answer; I shall get more customers through you than my neighbour by his giant, and you will get many presents.'

The little man felt quite indignant at the proposal of serving as a decoy to a barber. But was he not obliged to submit patiently to this insulting offer? He therefore quietly told the barber he had no time for such services, and went away.

Although the evil hag had thus stunted his growth, yet she had had no power to affect his mind, as he felt full well; for he no longer thought and felt as he did seven years since, and believed that he had become wiser and more sensible in the

interval.   He did not mourn for the loss of
his beauty, nor for his ugly appearance, but
only that he was driven from his father's
door like a dog.   However, he resolved to
make another trial with his mother.

He went again to her in the market, and
entreated her to listen to him patiently.
He reminded her of the day on which he
had gone with the old woman ; he called to
her mind all the particular incidents of his
childhood, told her then how he had served
seven years as a squirrel with the fairy, and
how she had changed him because he had
then ridiculed her person.

The cobbler's wife did not know what to
think of all this.   All that he related of his
childhood agreed with her own recollections,
but when he talked of serving seven years
as a squirrel she said, ' It is impossible ;
there are no fairies ; ' and when she looked
at him she felt a horror at the ugly dwarf,
and would not believe that he could be her
son.   At length she thought it would be
best to talk the matter over with her husband ; therefore she took up her baskets
and bade him go with her.

On arriving at the cobbler's stall she
said : ' Look, this fellow pretends to be our
lost Jacob.   He has told me all the circumstances ; how he was stolen from us seven
years since, and how he was enchanted by
a fairy.'

'Indeed,' interrupted the cobbler in a rage, 'has he told you this? wait, you rogue!—I have told him all this an hour ago, and then he goes to make a fool of you. Enchanted you have been, my little chap, have you? Wait a bit, I will soon disenchant you!' So saying, he took a bundle of straps that he had just cut, jumped up towards the dwarf, and beat him on his humped back and his long arms, making the little fellow scream with pain and run away crying.

Now in that town, as in others, there were but few of those compassionate souls who will support a poor unfortunate man who has a ridiculous appearance. Hence it was that the unlucky dwarf remained all day without food, and was obliged in the evening to choose for his night's quarters the steps of a church, though they were hard and cold.

When on the following morning the first rays of the sun awoke him, he began seriously to think how he should earn his livelihood, now that his father and mother had repudiated him; he was too proud to serve as a signboard to a barber; he would not hire himself as a merry-andrew to be exhibited: what then should he do? It now occurred to him that as a squirrel he had made considerable progress in the culinary art, and thought he might justly expect to prove a match for any cook ; he therefore resolved to turn his art to advantage.

As soon, therefore, as the morning had dawned, and the streets became animated, he entered a church and performed his devotions ; then he proceeded on his way. The duke (the sovereign of the country) was a notorious *gourmand*, who kept a good table, and sought cooks in all parts of the world. To his palace the dwarf went. When he arrived at the outer gate the porter asked his errand, and began to crack his jokes on him ; when he asked for the chief cook they laughed and led him through the inner courts, and wherever he went the servants stood still, looked at him, laughed heartily, and followed him, so that in a short time a great posse of menials of all descriptions crowded up the steps of the palace. The grooms threw away their curry - combs, the running footmen ran with all their might, the carpet-spreaders ceased beating their carpets, all crowded and thronged around him, as though the enemy were at the gates, and the shouts of 'A dwarf, a dwarf ! have you seen the dwarf ?' filled the air.

At this moment the steward of the palace, with a furious countenance and a large whip in his hand, made his appearance at the door, crying, 'For Heaven's sake, ye hounds, what is all this uproar for? Do you not know that our gracious master is still asleep?' At the same time he flourished his whip, laying it rather roughly about the backs of some grooms and porters.

'Why, sir,' they all cried, 'don't you see that we are bringing a dwarf, such a dwarf as you never saw?' The steward suppressed a loud laugh with difficulty when he got sight of the little man, for he was afraid that laughter would take from his dignity. He drove them all away with his whip except the dwarf, whom he led into the house and asked what he wanted. Hearing that the little man wished to see the master of the kitchen, he replied, 'You make a mistake, my little son; I suppose you want to see me, the steward of the palace, do you not? You wish to become dwarf to the duke, is it not so?'

'No, sir,' replied the dwarf, 'I am a clever cook and skilled in the preparation of all sorts of choice meats; be so kind as to bring me to the master of the kitchen; perhaps he may be in want of my skill.'

'Every one according to his wish, my little man; but you are an inconsiderate youth. To the kitchen! why, as the duke's dwarf you would have nothing to do and plenty to eat and drink to your heart's desire, and fine clothes into the bargain.

But we shall see ; your skill in the culinary
art will hardly be such as a cook to the
duke is required to possess, and you are
too good for a scullion.' As he said the
last words he took the dwarf by the hand
and conducted him to the apartments of the
master of the kitchen.

On arriving there the dwarf said, with
so deep a bow that his nose touched the
floor, ' Gracious sir, are you in want of a
skilful cook ? '

The master of the kitchen, surveying
him from top to toe, burst into a loud fit
of laughter, and said, ' What, you a cook ?
Do you think that our hearths are so low
that you could even look on one, though
you should stand on tiptoe, and stretch
your head ever so much out of your
shoulders ? My good little fellow, whoever
sent you here to hire yourself out as cook
has been making a fool of you.' Thus
saying, the master-cook laughed heartily,
and was joined by the steward of the palace
and all the servants in the room.

But the dwarf was not to be discomposed
by this. ' Of what consequence is it to
waste a few eggs, a little syrup and wine,
some flour and spice upon trial in a house
where there is plenty ? Give me some
dainty dish to prepare,' said he, ' procure
all that is necessary for it, and it shall be
immediately prepared before your eyes, so

that you shall be constrained to avow that I am a first-rate cook.'

While the dwarf was saying all this, and many other things, it was strange to see how his little eyes sparkled, how his long nose moved to and fro, and his fingers, which were like spiders' legs, suited their movements to his words.

'Well!' exclaimed the master-cook, taking the steward by the arm, 'Well! be it so for the sake of the joke, let us go to the kitchen.'

They walked through several large rooms and corridors till they came to the kitchen. This was a large spacious building magnificently fitted up; on twenty hearths fires were constantly burning, clear water was flowing through the midst, serving also as a fish-pond; in cupboards of marble and choice wood the stores were piled, which it was necessary to have at hand for use, and on either side were ten rooms, in which were kept all the delicious dainties for the palate which can be obtained in all the countries of Europe and in the East. Servants of all descriptions were running to and fro, handling and rattling kettles and pans, with forks and ladles; but when the master-cook entered all stood motionless, and the crackling of the fire and the rippling of the brook were alone heard.

'What has the duke ordered for breakfast

this morning?' he asked an old cook, who always prepared the breakfast.

'Sir, His Highness has pleased to order the Danish soup, with the small red Hamburg dumplings.'

'Well,' continued the master-cook, 'did you hear what the duke wishes to eat? Are you bold enough to attempt this difficult dish? At all events the dumplings you will not be able to make; that is quite a secret.'

'Nothing easier than that,' replied the dwarf, to their astonishment; for he had often made this dish when he was a squirrel. 'Nothing easier, only give me the herbs, the spices, fat of a wild boar, roots and eggs for the soup; but for the dumplings,' said he in a low voice, so that only the master-cook and the breakfast-maker could hear, 'for the dumplings I want various meats, wine, duck's fat, ginger, and the herb called the stomach comforter.'

'Ah, by St. Benedict, to what enchanter have you been apprenticed?' cried the cook in astonishment. 'You have hit all to a hair, and as to the noted herb, we did not know of that ourselves; yes! that must make the dish still more delicious. Oh! you miracle of a cook!'

'I should never have expected this,' said the master-cook, 'but let us make the trial; give him all he asks for, and let him prepare the breakfast.'

His orders were obeyed, and the necessary preparations were made on the hearth ;
but they now found that the dwarf could
not reach it.   They therefore put two chairs
together, laid a slab of marble on them,
and asked the little wonder to step up and
show his skill.   In a large circle stood the
cooks,   scullions,   servants,   and   others,
looking at him in amazement, seeing how
readily and quickly he proceeded, and how
cleanly and neatly he prepared everything.
When he had finished he ordered both
dishes to be put to the fire, and to be
boiled until he should call out ; then he
began to count one, two, three, and so on
up to five hundred, when he cried out,
' Stop, take them off,' and then invited the
head cook to taste them.

The taster ordered the scullion to bring
him a gold spoon, which he first rinsed in
the brook, and then gave it to the head
cook.   The latter, stepping up to the
hearth with a grave mien, took a spoonful, tasted it, and shutting his eyes,
smacked his lips with delight, saying,
' Delicious ! by the duke's life, delicious !
Would you not like to taste a spoonful,
Mr. Steward ?'   The latter, bowing, took
the spoon, tasted it, and was beside himself with delight.

' With all due respect to your skill, dear
breakfast-maker, you aged and experienced

cook, you have never been able to make soup or dumplings so delicious.'

The cook also tasted it, shook the dwarf reverentially by the hand, saying, ' My little man, you are a master of your art ; yes, that herb " stomach comforter " imparts a peculiar charm to the whole.'

At this moment the duke's valet entered the kitchen and informed them that the duke wished his breakfast. The preparations were now dished up on silver, and sent up to the duke ; but the head cook took the dwarf to his own room to converse with him. They had scarcely sat down long enough to say half a paternoster when a messenger came and called the head cook to the duke. He quickly put on his best clothes, and followed the messenger.

The duke looked well pleased. He had eaten all they had served, and was just wiping his beard as the master-cook entered. ' Master,' said he, ' I have hitherto always been well satisfied with your cooks ; but tell me who prepared the breakfast this morning ? It never was so delicious since I sat on the throne of my fathers ; tell me the name of the cook, that I may send him a ducat as a present.'

' My lord, this is a strange story,' replied the master ; and he told the duke that a dwarf had been brought to him that morning, who earnestly solicited the place

M

of a cook, and how all had happened. The duke was greatly astonished, ordered the dwarf to appear, and asked him who he was, and whence he came. Now poor Jacob did not exactly wish to say that he had been enchanted, and had served as a squirrel. But yet he adhered to truth, telling him that he now had neither father nor mother, and had learned cooking of an old woman. Much amused by the strange appearance of his new cook, the duke asked no more questions, but said, 'If you wish to remain here, I will give you fifty ducats a year, a suit of livery, and two pair of breeches beside. Your duty shall be to prepare my breakfast yourself every day, to give directions how the dinner shall be prepared, and to take the general superintendence of the cooking. As each in my palace has his proper name, you shall be called "Nose," and hold the office of sub-master-cook.'

The dwarf prostrated himself before the mighty duke, kissed his feet, and promised to serve him faithfully.

Thus the dwarf was for the present provided for, and did honour to his office. And it must be remarked that the duke had become quite an altered man since Nose, the dwarf, had been in the palace. Formerly, he had often been pleased to throw the dishes and plates that were served up at the heads of the cooks ; indeed, he even once, in a fit of rage, threw a fried calf's foot that was not sufficiently tender with such violence at the head of the master-cook that the latter fell to the ground, and was compelled for three days to keep his bed. 'Tis true the duke made him amends for what he had done by some handfuls of ducats, but still no cook ever came before him with his dishes without trembling and terror.

Ever since the dwarf had been in the palace all seemed to be changed, as if by magic. The duke, instead of three, now had five meals a day, in order to relish properly the skill of his little servant, and yet he never showed the least sign of discontent. Indeed, he found all new and excellent, was kind and pleasant, and became fatter every day.

He would often in the midst of a meal send for the master-cook and the dwarf, set one on his right, and the other on his left hand, and put with his own gracious fingers some morsels of the delicious viands into their mouths : a favour which both knew how to appreciate fully. The dwarf was the wonder of the whole town, and people requested the permission of the master-cook to see him cook, while some of the principal folks prevailed upon the duke to permit their servants to profit by the instructions of the dwarf in his kitchen, by which he obtained much money, for those who came to learn paid daily half a ducat. In order, however, to keep the other cooks in good humour, and prevent jealousy, Nose let them have the money that was paid by the masters for instruction.

Thus Nose lived almost two years in great comfort and honour, the thought of his parents alone saddening him, and nothing remarkable occurring until the following circumstance happened. The dwarf being particularly clever, and fortunate in his purchases, went himself, as often as time permitted, to the market, to buy poultry and fruit. One morning he went to the poultry-market, and walking up and down inquired for fat geese such as his master liked. His appearance, far from creating laughter and ridicule, commanded respect, since he was known as the duke's celebrated cook, and each poultry-woman felt herself happy if he but turned his nose to her. At length coming to the end of a row of stalls, he perceived in a corner a woman with geese for sale, who did not, like the others, praise her goods, nor call to the customers.

He stepped up to her, examined the geese, weighed them in his hand, and finding them to his liking, bought three, with the cage they were in, put them on his shoulders, and trotted home. It appeared singular to him that only two of the geese cackled and cried like others, the third being quite quiet and thoughtful, and occasionally groaning and moaning like a human being.

'She is not well,' said he to himself; 'I must hasten to get home and dress her.' But the goose replied, distinctly,

> 'If thou stick'st me,
> Why I'll bite thee,
> And if my neck thou twistest round,
> Thou soon wilt lie below the ground.'

Quite startled, the dwarf put down the basket, and the goose, looking at him with her fine intelligent eyes, sighed. 'Why, what have we here?' cried Nose. 'You can talk, Miss Goose. I never expected that. Well, make yourself easy; I know the world and will not harm so rare a bird. But I would wager something that you have not always been covered with feathers. Indeed I was once a poor squirrel myself.'

'You are right,' replied the goose, 'in saying I was not born with this disgraceful disguise. Alas! it was never sung at my cradle that Mimi, the great Wetterbock's daughter, would be killed in the kitchen of a duke.'

'Pray be easy, dear Miss Mimi,' said the dwarf, comforting her, 'for as sure as I am an honest fellow, and sub-master-cook to His Highness, no one shall touch your throat. I will give you a stall in my own apartments,

you shall have enough food, and I will de-
vote my leisure time to converse with 'you.
I'll tell the others in the kitchen that I am
fattening a goose with various herbs for the
duke, and at the first opportunity you shall
be set at liberty.'

The goose thanked him with tears in her
eyes, and the dwarf, as he had promised,
killed the other two geese, but built a stall
for Mimi, under the pretence of preserving
her for some special occasion.   Instead of
feeding her on grain he gave her pastry and
sweetmeats.   As often as he had time he
went to converse with her and comfort her.
They related their histories to each other,
and Nose learnt that she was the daughter
of the enchanter, Wetterbock, who lived in
the island of Gothland.   Being involved in
a quarrel with an old fairy, her father had
been conquered by stratagems and cunning,
and out of revenge the fairy had changed
her into a goose, and brought her to the
town.

When the dwarf told his history she said,
' I am not inexperienced in these matters,
my father having given me and my sisters
what instruction he was allowed to impart.
The story of the dispute at your mother's
fruit stall, your sudden metamorphosis when
you smelled the herb, as well as the words
the old woman used, show me that you are
enchanted through herbs ; that is to say, if

you can find out the herb of which the fairy
thought when she bewitched you, you may
be disenchanted.' This was but poor conso-
lation for the dwarf, for how should he find
the herb? Yet he thanked her and felt
some hope.

About this time the duke had a visit from
a neighbouring prince, his friend. He,
therefore, ordered the dwarf to appear, and
said, 'Now is the time for you to show
whether you serve me faithfully and are
master of your art. The prince, who is now
visiting me, keeps the best table after me,
as is well known. He is a great connoisseur
in good living, and a wise man. Let it now
be your care to supply my table every day
so that his astonishment shall daily become
greater. But you must not, under pain of
my displeasure, repeat the same dish during
his visit. You may ask of my treasurer all
you want, and should it be needful to fry
gold and diamonds you must do it. I would
rather become poor than forfeit his good
opinion of my taste.'

When the duke had concluded the dwarf
bowed most respectfully, saying, 'Be it as
you say, my lord; please God I shall do
all to gratify the palate of this prince of
gourmands.'

The little cook now mustered all his skill.
He did not spare his master's treasures, and
still less did he spare himself. He was seen

all day at the fire, enveloped by clouds of smoke, and his voice constantly resounded through the vaults of the kitchen, for he governed the scullions and under-cooks.

During a fortnight the foreign prince lived happily, and feasted sumptuously with the duke. They ate not less than five times a day, and the duke was delighted with his dwarf, seeing satisfaction expressed on the countenance of his guest. But on the fifteenth day it happened that the duke, while at table, sent for the dwarf, presented him to his guest, and asked how he was satisfied with his cooking?

'You are a wonderful cook,' replied the prince, 'and know what good living is. All the time I have been here you have not repeated a single dish, and have prepared everything exquisitely. But pray tell me, why have you not all this time prepared that queen of dishes, the pie called "souzeraine"?'

The dwarf was startled at this question, for he had never heard of this queen of pies; however, he recovered himself and replied, 'My lord, I was in hopes that your serene countenance would shine some time yet on this court, therefore I deferred this dish; for with what dish but the queen of pies should the cook honour the day of your departure?'

'Indeed!' said the duke, laughing, 'I

suppose then you wish to wait for the day of my death to honour me, for you have never yet sent it up to me. But think of another dish to celebrate the departure, for to-morrow that pie must be on the table.'

'Your pleasure shall be done, my lord,' replied the dwarf, and retired. But he went away uneasy, for the day of his disgrace and misfortune had come. He did not know how to prepare this pie. He went therefore to his chamber and wept over his fate, when the goose Mimi, who was allowed to walk about, came up and inquired the cause of his grief. When she heard of the pie, 'Dry your tears,' said she, 'this dish often came to my father's table, and I know pretty well what is necessary for it ; you have only to take such and such things in certain quantities, and should these not be all that are really necessary, I trust that the taste of these gentlemen is not sufficiently refined to discover the deficiency.'

At these words the dwarf danced with joy, blessed the day on which he had purchased the goose, and set about making this queen of pies. He first made a trial in miniature, and lo ! the flavour was exquisite, and the master-cook, to whom he gave the small pie to taste, praised his great skill once more.

The following day he prepared the pie on a larger scale, and, after having garnished it with flowers, sent it hot as it came from

the oven to table.   After which he dressed
in his best and went to the dining-hall.   On
entering he found the steward engaged in
carving the pie, and presenting it on silver
dishes to the duke and his guest.   The duke
swallowed a large piece, turned his eyes
upward, saying ' Ha ! ha ! ha ! justly is this
called the queen of pies ; but my dwarf is
also a king of cooks.   Is it not so, my
friend ? '

His guest took a small morsel, tasted it
carefully, and smiled somewhat scornfully
and mysteriously.

' The thing is made pretty well,' he replied,
pushing his plate away, ' but it is not quite
the Souzeraine, as I well imagined.'

At this the duke frowned with indigna-
tion, and turned red, saying, ' You hound
of a dwarf, how dare you do this to your
lord ?   I will have your big head cut off as
a punishment for your bad cooking.'

' Ah, my lord,' said the dwarf, trembling,
' for Heaven's sake have compassion on me ;
I have made that dish, indeed, according to
the proper receipt, and am sure that nothing
is wanting.'

' 'Tis a lie, you knave,' replied the duke,
giving him a kick, ''tis a lie, else my guest
would not say there was something wanting.
I will have you yourself cut up and baked
in a pie.'

' Have compassion on me ! ' exclaimed

the dwarf, shuffling on his knees up to the
prince, and clasping his feet ; 'tell me what
is wanting to this pie and why it does not
suit your palate : let me not die for a handful of meat or flour.'

' This will not avail you, my good Nose,'
replied the prince, laughing ; 'even yester-
day I thought you would not be able to make
this dish as well as my cook.   Know there
is wanting a herb called Sneeze-with-pleasure,
which is not even known in this country.
Without it this pie is insipid, and your
master will never eat it in such perfection
as I do.'

At this the duke flew into a rage, and
cried with flashing eyes :

' I will eat it in perfection yet, for I swear
by my princely honour that by to-morrow I
will either have the pie set before you, such
as you desire it, or the head of this fellow
shall be spiked on the gate of my palace.
Go, you hound, I give you once more twenty-
four hours !' cried the duke.

The dwarf again went to his chamber and
mourned over his fate with the goose that
he must die, as he had never heard of this
herb.   'If it is nothing more,' said she, 'I
can help you out of the difficulty, as my
father has taught me to know all herbs.   At
any other time your death, no doubt, would
have been certain, and it is fortunate for you
that we have a new moon, as the herb is

only then in flower.   Now tell me, are there
any old chestnut-trees in the neighbourhood
of the palace ? '

'Oh yes,' replied Nose with a lighter
heart, 'near the lake, about two hundred
yards from the palace, there is a clump of
them ; but what of them ? '

'Why,' said Mimi, 'the herb only flowers
at the foot of them.   Now let us lose no
time but go to fetch what you want ; take
me on your arm, and put me down when
we get out, that I may search for you.'

He did as she requested, and went towards
the gate of the palace, but here the porter
levelled his gun and said: 'My good Nose, it
is all over with you ; you must not pass ; I
have strict orders respecting you.'

'But I suppose I may go into the garden,'
replied the dwarf.   'Be so good as to send
one of your fellow-servants to the master of
the palace, and ask whether I may not go
into the garden to fetch herbs.'   The porter
did so and permission was given, since, the
garden having high walls, escape was impossible.   But when Nose and Mimi had
got out he put her carefully down, and she
ran quickly before him towards the lake,
where the chestnuts were.   He followed
with a heavy heart, since this was his last
and only hope.   If she did not find the
herb he was resolved rather to plunge into
the lake than to have his head cut off.   The

goose searched in vain under all the chestnut-trees ; she turned every herb with her
beak, but no trace of the one wanted was to
be found, and she now began to cry out of
compassion and fear for the dwarf, as the
evening was already growing dusk, and the
objects around were difficult to distinguish.

At this moment the dwarf cast a glance
across the lake, and cried suddenly : ' Look,
look, yonder across the lake there stands a
large old tree ; let us go there and search ;
perhaps my luck may bloom there.' The
goose hopped and flew before him, and he
ran after her as quickly as his short legs
would permit him ; the chestnut-tree cast
a large shade, and it was so dark around
that scarcely anything could be distinguished ;
but suddenly the goose stopped, flapped her
wings for joy, put her head quickly into the
high grass, and plucked something which
she reached gracefully with her bill to the
astonished Nose, saying, ' There is the
herb, and plenty is growing here, so that
you will never want for it.'

The dwarf looked thoughtfully at the herb,
and a sweet odour arose from it, which immediately reminded him of the scene of his
metamorphosis ; the stalk and leaves were
of a bluish green, bearing a glowing red
flower, with a yellow edge.

' God be praised !' he now exclaimed,
' what a miracle ! I believe this is the very

herb that transformed me from a squirrel into this hideous form ; shall I make a trial, to see what effect it will have on me ?'

'Not yet,' entreated the goose. 'Take a handful of this herb with you ; let us go to your room and put up all the money and whatever you have, and then we will try the virtue of the herb.'

They did so, and went again to his room, the dwarf's heart beating audibly with anticipation. After having put up about fifty or sixty ducats which he had saved, he tied up his clothes in a bundle, and said : 'If it please God, I shall get rid of my burthensome deformity.' He then put his nose deep into the herb and inhaled its odour.

Now his limbs began to stretch and crack, he felt how his head started from his shoulders, he squinted down on his nose and saw how it became smaller and smaller, his back and chest became straight, and his legs longer.

The goose viewed all this with great astonishment, exclaiming, 'Ah, what a tall handsome fellow you have now become. God be praised, there is no trace left in you of what you were before.' Now Jacob was highly rejoiced ; he folded his hands and prayed. But his joy did not make him forget what he owed to Mimi the goose ; his heart indeed urged him to go to his parents, yet from gratitude he overcame his wish and

said, 'To whom but to you am I indebted
that I am again restored to my former self?
Without you I should never have found this
herb, but should have continued for ever in
that form, or else have died under the axe
of the executioner.   Well, I will repay you.
I will bring you back to your father; he
being so experienced in magic will be able
easily to disenchant you.'

The goose shed tears of joy and accepted
his offer.   Jacob fortunately escaped unknown from the palace with his goose, and
started on his way for the sea-coast towards
Mimi's home.

It is needless to add that their journey
was successful, that Wetterbock disenchanted
his daughter, and dismissed Jacob laden
with presents, that the latter returned to his
native town, that his parents with delight
recognised in the handsome young man their
lost son, that he, with the presents that he
had received, purchased a shop and became
wealthy and happy.

Only this much may be added, that after
his departure from the duke's palace there
was great consternation, for when, on the
next morning, the duke was about to fulfil
his oath, and to have the dwarf beheaded in
case he had not discovered the herbs, he
was nowhere to be found; and the prince
maintained that the duke had let him escape
secretly rather than lose his best cook, and

accused him of breaking his word of honour. This circumstance gave rise to a great war between the two princes, which is well known in history by the name of the 'Herb War.' Many battles were fought, but at length a peace was concluded, which is now called the 'Pie Peace,' because at the festival of reconciliation the Souzeraine, queen of pies, was prepared by the prince's cook, and relished by the duke in the highest degree.

Thus the most trifling causes often lead to the greatest result ; and this, reader, is the story of ' Nose, the Dwarf.'

THE END

Printed by R. & R. CLARK, *Edinburgh*